Slack

Slack

Getting Past Burnout, Busywork, and the Myth of Total Efficiency

Tom DeMarco

BROADWAY BOOKS

New York

BROADWAY

Broadway Books titles may be purchased for business or promotional use or for special sales. For information, please write to: Special Markets Department, Random House, Inc., 1540 Broadway, New York, NY 10036.

BROADWAY BOOKS and its logo, a letter B bisected on the diagonal, are trademarks of Broadway Books, a division of Random House, Inc.

Visit our website at www.broadwaybooks.com

Library of Congress Cataloging-in-Publication Data

DeMarco, Tom.
Slack : getting past burnout, busywork, and the myth of total efficiency /
Tom DeMarco.
      p.   cm.
1. Industrial management.   2. Job stress.   3. Risk management.   I. Title.
HD31.D4222 2001
658—dc21
00-065109

First Edition

Designed by Paul Randall Mize

ISBN 0-7679-0768-x

10   9   8   7   6   5   4   3   2   1

In memory of
Murray Ogden Smyth (1904–2000)

Acknowledgments

Thanks to my editor, Suzanne Oaks, and editorial assistant, Claire Johnson, at Broadway Books for help in preparing *Slack* for publication. I particularly value the patient guidance they offered about changes required for the work to be able to fulfill its promise. Thanks as well to my agents Emma Parry and Michael Carlisle of Carlisle and Company for help in finding the perfect publisher.

The ideas and philosophies that make up *Slack* did not come to me out of a vacuum. They were formed and tested over years of interaction with clients and coworkers. Thanks to all of them. For specific insights and (just as important) useful ways to articulate them, I owe a special debt to my colleagues at the Atlantic Systems Guild: Peter Hruschka, Steve McMenamin, John Palmer, James Robertson, and Suzanne Robertson. Each has contributed at least one thing to the book. I am particularly indebted to Tim Lister, who, over the course of nearly twenty-five years of close interaction, has helped to shape my thinking on most aspects of organizational life. (He has sometimes made me go, "Ahah!" so hard it hurt my chest.) Thanks as well to Rob Austin, James Bach, Sheila Brady, Karen Coburn, Allan DeMarco, Ernst Denert, Lesley DeVoe, Rose Ann

Giordano, Jim Highsmith, Norm Kerth, Jut Kodner, Ken Orr, Sally O. Smyth, Bruce Taylor, John Taylor, Jerry Weinberg, and Ed Yourdon for ideas and phrasings and nuances that made their way into the pages of *Slack*.

—Tom DeMarco

Contents

Prelude

Slack is a prescription for building a capacity to change into the modern enterprise. It looks into the heart of the efficiency-flexibility quandary: The more efficient you get, the harder it is to change. The book shows managers how to make their organizations slightly less efficient but enormously more effective. It coaches them on the introduction of *slack*, the missing ingredient required for all change. It counsels a thoughtful use of slack instead of the mindless obsession with elimination of all slack in the interests of efficiency.

Why Now?

We live in an age of acceleration. Whatever the formula was for business success a few years ago, it won't work today. Today there needs to be more and more work crammed into less and less time. There are fewer people doing more and doing it faster in less space with less support and with tighter tolerances and higher quality requirements than ever before. The average manager or knowledge worker is so busy today that there is simply not a spare moment for anything. There isn't time to plan, only to do. There is no time for analysis, invention, training, strategic thinking, contemplation, or lunch.

Only a decade ago, the workplace was characterized by "bankers' hours," conversations around a water cooler, extended business meals, early closings in summer, and the corporate softball league. Today such things have gone the way of the milkman and the full-service gas station.

The ubiquitous Hurry Up mantra of business today has undoubtedly helped corporations speed up. They do what they do faster and more cheaply than before. But there is a downside . . .

Enter the Need for Change

Suppose that what the corporation is doing now has to be changed. The needed change is not just to do the same things still faster but to switch directions and do something else entirely. Change is always complicated and challenging, but in the superaccelerated corporation, change of direction is almost impossible. The very improvements that the Hurry Up organization has made to go faster and cheaper have undermined its capacity to make any other kind of change.

An organization that can accelerate but not change direction is like a car that can speed up but not steer. In the short run, it makes lots of progress in whatever direction it happened to be going. In the long run, it's just another road wreck.

Plan of the Book

The book is divided into four parts, each with its own mini-theme:

Part One   Slack: The unfortunate tradeoff between efficiency and flexibility. How organizations tend to get more efficient only by sacrificing their ability to change. How slack can come to the rescue.

Part Two   The effect of stress on organizations: It leads them badly off course while causing them to redouble their speed. Causes of and cures for corporate stress.

Part Three Change, growth, and organizational learning: The difference between companies that can learn (and profit from their learning), and those that can't.

Part Four Risk taking and risk management: Why running away from risk is a no-win strategy, and why running *toward* it makes sense when managed sensibly (and what that entails).

Slack is directed toward management at all levels in knowledge organizations and other modern corporations where knowledge workers predominate. It is also directed to the knowledge workers themselves. It's directed toward you if you sense that there is something terribly wrong in the infernal busyness of the modern workplace, if you know in your heart that the slack that has been squeezed out of your organizations over the last ten years now has to be reintroduced, or no further meaningful progress will ever be possible.

The fact that you've decided to read this book says that you are *busy*. You haven't got time for an extended treatise on organizational forms or a theory of management. At most, you may have the time for a very fast, very pointed airplane read. I have put this book together so it can be read cover-to-cover on a flight from New York to Chicago or from Amsterdam to Rome. It is my hope and expectation that after reading it, you can step off your flight with a straightforward approach for helping your organization make the kinds of change it will need to make in order to survive.

Benefits of Slack

Reduced stress and reintroduction of an essential bit of slack is my best recipe for:

❑ Increased organizational agility
❑ Better retention of key personnel (what I call your "human capital")
❑ An improved ability to invest in the future
❑ A capacity for sensible risk taking instead of risk avoidance

In an earlier age, when you had a bit of free time on your hands, you might have occasionally played around with a little puzzle game like the one pictured to the right. The object of the game is to slide the numbered tiles successively into the open space, in order to effect a perfect ordering.

Getting the tiles into order is a distinctly nontrivial exercise. It's hard enough with the game in its traditional form. But now consider a modified—dare I say improved?—form such as the one shown on the next page.

Now instead of eight tiles and one open space, we have a game with nine tiles and no open space. The efficiency of this layout is improved by 11.1 percent, since the waste space is gone, and all the squares are 100 percent in use. (Chances are that as you read these words, someone in your organization is applying the same logic to the office and seating plan.) Efficiency is improved, but something else is lost. Without the

Note how efficiency
is increased by
use of waste space!

open space, there is no further possibility of moving tiles at all.
The layout may be optimal as it is, but if time proves otherwise,
there is no way to change it.

The open space represents what I call *slack,* the degree of
freedom required to effect change. Slack is the natural enemy
of efficiency, and efficiency is the natural enemy of slack. And
there is the rub: There are things you can do to make an organization more efficient that interfere with its ability to
change and reinvent itself later.

For the moment, I propose that you consider the nine-tile
game (with no open space) to be a symbol of your organization: improved, restructured, efficient as all get-out . . . but no
longer able to change.

1

Madmen in the Halls

THE LEGACY of the nineties has been a dangerous corporate delusion: the idea that organizations are effective only to the extent that all their workers are totally and eternally busy. Anyone who's not overworked (sweating, staying late, racing from one task to the next, working Saturdays, unable to squeeze time for even the briefest meeting till two weeks after next) is looked on with suspicion. People with a little idle time on their hands may not even be safe. As one of my friends at Digital Equipment Corporation told me during the company's darkest days, "There are madmen in the halls, looking for someone to ax." Of course, the ones they were looking to ax were the folks who weren't all that busy.

Crisis of Confidence

Your company may not now have actual ax-wielding crazies roaming the halls, but their specter is almost certainly still with you. This is the remnant of the crisis of confidence we've just come through. Consider: As this is being written, American and western European business is in a period of extraordinary prosperity. The rest of the world is a basket case and we are healthier than we've ever been. And yet just a few short years ago, we were all in an agony of doubt. How could we survive, we wondered, against the competition of the ravenous third world, willing to work for peanuts and liable to undersell us in any market anywhere? How could we stay even with the superbly educated Japanese, or those clever and hungry workers coming out from behind the Iron Curtain, or the Taiwanese and Koreans with their superhuman work ethic and their awesome skills? Acting on our doubts, we went through a purge of excess capacity (i.e., people with homes and families). We trimmed as though our very survival depended on trimming.

Wasn't it reasonable to put our house in order in this fashion? Maybe it was in the short run. It probably contributed at least somewhat to our present strength. Yet the lasting side effect of the purge—the notion that busyness is the essence of business—can only do us long-term harm.

The Price of "Putting Our House in Order"

During the last ten years we have downsized, "right-sized," laid off, and fired people's butts. We have cut payrolls, closed plants, sold off divisions, and generally scared all our remaining employees to death. We nodded in approval as characters like Chainsaw Al (at one time the worst CEO in America) did their dirty work. We bid up the stocks of companies like AT&T who led the trend, i.e., led the retreat.

The principal target of the cuts has been that bugaboo of organizational efficiency: middle management. We asked ourselves, "What are they, after all, those middle managers? What are they but fat? What do they really exist for other than to be

cut out in the interest of efficiency?" And so we cut. We surgi-
cally removed the middle layers of our organizations, flattening
the charts and widening the scope of management at each
level.

We went from this: to this:

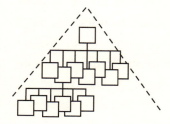 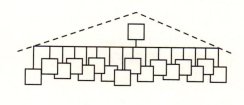

Was that a good thing to do? I have my doubts.

Maybe middle management exists for some reason above
and beyond filling the space between the top and the bottom
of the hierarchy. Part of my purpose in this book is to examine
what's supposed to happen in the middle of a healthy organization, the critical role of middle management.

The main activity of those managers is *reinvention*. It is the
middle of the organization where reinvention takes place. This
is where the dynamic of today's organizational functioning is
examined, taken apart, analyzed, resynthesized, and assembled
back into new organizational models that allow us to move for-
ward.

What got cut out of the most aggressively purged organizations is the capacity to change. The so-called restructurings
have, in most cases, optimized the present steady state, only at
the expense of the future.

Does It Matter?

Well, so what? Some companies have always been prone to
trade away the future to make the present look a little more

rosy. In the short term they prosper, and in the long term they don't. What's different this time? The difference is that today even the companies that didn't cut the heart out of their effective change centers have made it more difficult for those centers to operate. Change and reinvention require a commodity that is absent in our time as it never has been before. That commodity—the catalytic ingredient of all change—is slack. Slack is the time when reinvention happens. It is time when you are not 100 percent busy doing the operational business of your firm. Slack is the time when you are 0 percent busy.

Slack at all levels is necessary to make the organization work effectively and to grow. It is the lubricant of change. Good companies excel in the creative use of slack. And bad ones can only obsess about removing it.

2
Busyness

IMAGINE that you took on an assignment to direct a film about happenings inside a hugely successful company. How would you portray the company? How, in particular, would you make it *look* successful? One tempting answer is to convey its great success by showing everyone who works there to be immensely busy all the time. After all, you might reason, how would the company have become so successful if its people weren't putting in substantial extra effort?

My own experience consulting inside some highly successful companies (Microsoft, Apple, Hewlett-Packard, IBM, Dupont, to name a few) cannot corroborate a relationship between busyness and success. Very successful companies have never struck me as particularly busy; in fact, they are, as a group, rather laid-back. Energy is evident in the workplace, but it's not the energy tinged with fear that comes from being slightly behind on everything. The companies I have come to admire most show little obvious sense of hurry. They are more like an extended family, embarked upon a project whose goal is only partly expressed in getting something done; the other part of the goal is that all involved learn and grow and enjoy themselves along the way.

Work, particularly knowledge work, can be extremely enjoyable. That's why so many of us become addicted to it. If you take sensual pleasure in your work, and those around you are doing the same thing, if it's clearly okay in your corporate culture to enjoy what you're doing, chances are that yours is a company headed toward success. Sign up for the stock plan.

The Busy Worker

Extreme busyness is injurious to the real work of the organization. I will make that point as carefully as I can in the chapters to follow, stressing the effect in particular on management. But first, I ask you to consider how busyness may hurt the effectiveness of even the lowest-level workers.

Take, for example, the secretary. (You remember secretaries, don't you? A once-common element of corporate life.) A secretary's job may involve document preparation, appointment scheduling, coordinating, and generally facilitating the smooth functioning of one manager's work life—let's say yours. We'll call her Sylvia.

A good secretary is a treasure, as anyone who has ever worked with one knows, and Sylvia is definitely a treasure. With Sylvia around, everything goes more smoothly. When you're away from the office—it never looks this way officially, but whom are we kidding?—Sylvia is effectively in charge. She is the one who coordinates and distributes work to be done. If she ever left, it would set you and your organization back a few months, at least.

But now into this happy scenario drop a consultant with a charter to reduce cost, the "corporate restructuring agent."

Whoa, he says, what's this? A secretary? And what's she up to this very minute? He parks himself beside Sylvia's desk with his trusty stopwatch in hand. To no one's surprise, he finds that Sylvia is really only busy 43 percent of the time. The rest of the time she is . . . available. She's available to do stuff that you or your people find you need to have done. That's part of what's so great about Sylvia: When something comes up, she can usually get cracking on it right away.

A look of triumph now comes over the consultant's face. If Sylvia is only busy 43 percent of the time, 57 percent of her cost is potentially savable. Why, all we have to do is dump Sylvia into a "pool" and allocate 43 percent of her time to you and the rest to other people. Or have you share her with some other manager who needs only 57 percent of a full person. Or even get rid of Sylvia entirely and hire a temp for that 43 percent of the time that you really need someone. (You can be sure that the consultant will be checking back later to find out if you *really* need that much help.)

What an improvement. Sylvia's gone or gone 57 percent of the time, and 57 percent of what she was costing the organization goes directly down to the bottom line. Wow. In place of a person who was idle 57 percent of the time, we now have someone who is busy 100 percent of the time. Talk about efficiency!

The problem, of course, is that the now-slackless secretary or portion thereof is simply not as responsive as Sylvia was. This highly efficient person doesn't get cracking right away on anything new that comes up, because this highly efficient person is too busy.

How We Work Together

Modern organizations are huge networks of interconnected work. The nodes of this network are you and your coworkers.

The connections are pieces of work in progress that get passed from one person to another.

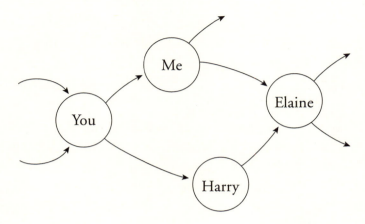

As a practical matter it is impossible to keep everyone in the organization 100 percent busy unless we allow for some buffering at each employee's desk. That means there is an in-box where work stacks up.

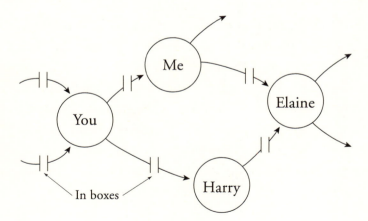

With enough buffer at each desk, the work flow can now be organized to keep everyone busy all the time.

A side effect of this optimally efficient scheme is that the net time for work to pass through the organization must necessarily increase. Think of it from the work's point of view: The time it takes to move entirely through the network is increased by each pause it has to make in someone's in-basket. If workers were available when the work arrived at their desks, there would be no wait and the total transit time would be reduced. But availability implies at least some inefficiency, and that's what our efficiency program has drummed out of the organization.

Making efficient use of workers in the sense of removing all slack from their day has an attendant cost in responsiveness and results directly in slowing the organization down. This is not an entirely happy tradeoff. As Bill Gates testified in the early proceedings of the Microsoft trial, "In the past, only the fittest would survive. Today, only the fastest will survive."

It's possible to make an organization more efficient without making it better. That's what happens when you drive out slack. It's also possible to make an organization a little less efficient and improve it enormously. In order to do that, you need to reintroduce enough slack to allow the organization to breathe, to reinvent itself, and to make necessary change.

3

The Myth of Fungible Resource

TYPICAL RESTRUCTURING EFFORTS concentrate on making a company more efficient. I have argued that the potential to do harm in this endeavor is substantial. In other words, improving efficiency may in many cases be countereffective. But that is not to imply that improving efficiency is therefore easy. It isn't. In fact, it takes a huge amount of work and real ingenuity. It's hard to make an organization more efficient because the workers of that organization have been constantly trying to make themselves more efficient. They've been doing that for years, since they are frustrated by waste and bored by idleness. The efficiency expert who now comes into the organization is obliged to plow over terrain that has been plowed over by many thoughtful persons before. Up against this daunting challenge, who can blame him if he takes the odd shortcut from time to time to show a little apparent progress?

The Oddest Shortcut of All

The tendency to shortcut is further encouraged by the sense—almost always present when restructuring is in the air—that *apparent* progress is every bit as good as *actual* progress. Dividing Sylvia between two bosses, for example, is only apparent progress, since her improved efficiency is offset by her reduced responsiveness. But if the efficiency expert has only a week to trim the fat . . . Well, you can understand the temptation.

So what's a useful shortcut for an efficiency expert who needs to show some quick organizational "improvement"? The shortcut that is most frequently employed is to assume that individual workers are entirely *fungible*.

> **fun·gi·ble** (fu´ jə bəl) *adj.* (especially of goods) being of such nature or kind as to be freely exchangeable or replaceable, in whole or in part, for another of like nature or kind.

Money is fungible, for example. You can take it out of one pile—say, "Maintenance"—and add it to another pile—say, "Groceries"—without any net loss in the transfer. Dollars out of Maintenance equals dollars into Groceries. The Maintenance dollars you transferred are no different from the Groceries dollars that were there already. They all spend the same. Money is fungible . . . but people aren't.

If you are an efficiency expert under the gun, you can see how appealing it is to assume that people are fungible. That allows you to move people around freely to show an apparent productivity gain in no time at all. (Efficiency experts, after all, have to be efficient.) If a Sylvia can be treated as goods, capable of being divided up and "exchangeable or replaceable, in whole or in part" with other Sylvia-like workers, then assigning her 43 percent to one department and 57 percent to another makes perfect sense. If she's not a fungible resource, this makes no sense at all, so (shudder) just don't worry your little head about that possibility.

Matrix Management

The assumption of fungible humans has come into its own in that mainstay of organizational theory called *matrix management*. In a matrix-managed organization, each worker reports to two bosses. The boss drawn directly above the worker on the org chart is the functionally responsible manager, the person who gives that worker his or her marching orders. And the boss off on the side is the discipline manager, the one who is in

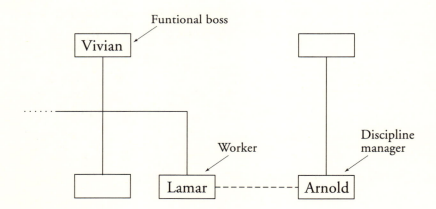

charge (in some sense) of all workers with the same or similar skill sets. In the figure, Lamar, a layout artist, reports to Vivian, his project manager, but also reports to Arnold, who manages all the designers and artists. In project-related matters, it's Vivian who is in charge. She decides what Lamar will be doing today and tomorrow. At raise time, though, it's up to Arnold to perform the review, and Arnold is also responsible for Lamar's training and advancement.

Half the world is so used to matrix management as to take the scheme for granted. The other half just thinks it's bizarre. How on earth, this second group might ask, does Arnold know how well Lamar has performed except by talking with his real boss, Vivian? She knows and Arnold doesn't, so why doesn't she do the review? The same might be said for making the decision that Lamar is ready for increased responsibilities. Matrix management doesn't make a huge amount of sense . . . until you hit upon the happy notion of treating Lamar as a totally fungible resource. That says he not only can be moved around freely but can be divided up.

In the next figure, we see Lamar involved on three different projects. Obviously, none of his bosses on the vertical can assemble a complete picture of how well Lamar is doing. Now at last there is a real need for Arnold.

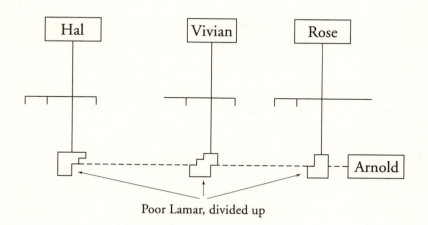

Poor Lamar, divided up

This kind of matrix management is particularly appealing when none of the vertical bosses has enough need to justify a person full-time. It's also handy when outside calls on a worker's time are varied; let the guy work full-time on his main job but then get matrixed out on an as-needed basis. Companies that adopt this approach think of themselves as agile and infinitely flexible.

Task-Switching Penalties

The problem is that human workers are not entirely fungible. Even the most dedicated advocate of matrix management will understand that there are limits to how many ways an individual can be divided. They might think it okay for Lamar to have two assignments, for example, but begin to feel queasy about five. And ten or more are obviously too many.

The reason ten are too many ways to split Lamar has to do with the cost he incurs in switching tasks. For example, if he's working on each of his tasks at least part of each day, then he has to make at least nine switches per day. If each switch uses up ten minutes (to put away one set of drawings and take out the other, find the right instruments and media, locate the job description and the notes from the last meeting), then ninety minutes of Lamar's day are lost to switching. Over an eight-hour day that works out to a nearly 20 percent penalty. That time is not spent productively on any one of his tasks; it is simply wasted.

This ten-minute task-switching penalty is used up on the mechanics alone of the change: putting stuff away and taking other stuff out. But depending on what kind of work Lamar is doing, the switching penalty may be far more substantial than that. Suppose he's not now in the drawing and layout phase of a project, but is conceptualizing. He is thinking out an ad campaign or concocting an interesting mix of images to convey a point. This rather mysterious activity is essential to his work, but not very well structured; Lamar himself probably couldn't divide conceptualization into component pieces or impose an order on its subtasks. That means that if he has to stop in the middle, he won't have a perfectly clean partitioning between work aborted today and restarted tomorrow. To get himself going tomorrow, he may have to go through some of the same mental steps that he's just been through today. This rework is added to the mechanical components of the task-partitioning penalty.

Even this may still be a too-optimistic model for what task switching really costs. There are certain kinds of work that require *immersion* into the task before progress can begin. In this category I include jobs like writing, research, analysis, invention, and programming. The immersion time is required to overcome a kind of mental inertia. Most of us are reluctant to begin on such a task unless we have a large block of time set aside.

There may also be emotional inertia to overcome in some tasks. You can imagine a nurse, for example, pausing with her hand on the doorknob of a patient's room, gathering her forces before a difficult procedure, or a salesperson building up confidence before a call.

When highly immersive tasks are interrupted, a second immersion period is required to get going again. There may also be a frustration component if interruption is frequent. Workers who are frustrated have to use up some of their energy and time to calm themselves and face up to the potential for further frustration when they begin again.

The waste associated with time-sharing between two tasks is the sum of time lost to the mechanics of the switch *plus* rework required upon restart *plus* immersion time *plus* frustration cost. You pay the penalty each time you switch.

Effect on Teams

Finally, switching may impose another kind of penalty, one that hurts your continuing productivity rather than just costing you a fixed amount of lost time. This occurs in tasks that are performed by people working in tightly knit teams. If you've ever worked on such a team, you know that there is a productivity boost due to "binding," the effect of adherence to a common goal. There is something about a team that energizes and focuses all the participants so that the whole of the team's capacity is greater than the sum of its parts. But teams tend to be obsessive by nature. A highly partitioned worker can't be obsessively involved in any of his/her many fragmented tasks, and so tends not to bind into the team. Whatever the productivity boost due to team action may be, the partitioned worker does not benefit from it.

The complete task-switching penalty is thus seen to include all of these components:

Task-switching penalty = Mechanics of moving to a new task +
Rework due to inopportune abort +
Immersion time for think-intensive
   tasks +
Frustration (emotional immersion) +
Loss of team binding effect

Task-Switching Penalty Quantified

So far, all I've done is list the components of a task-switching penalty. Let me now try to quantify their aggregate effect. In my experience, there is never less than a 15 percent penalty due to time-sharing a knowledge worker between two or more tasks. Moving a person who had been assigned to a single job to work part-time on a second exposes you to a loss of at least six hours per week of that person's time. And the penalty is greater when the partitioning is greater. I limit this statement to knowledge workers, since manual and blue-collar workers may not be affected, or may be less affected, by some of the components of the task-switching penalty. For knowledge workers, though, the minimum penalty is 15 percent.

The only method I have used so far to substantiate the 15 percent minimum penalty is a time-honored approach called *proof by repeated assertion*. Its conclusiveness rests on the fact that I have stated that there is a 15 percent minimum penalty and then stated it again (and again and again and again). Although widely used, proof by repeated assertion, you may argue, lacks a certain amount of satisfying rigor. To which I answer, "Compared to what?" Before I waded in, the presumption seemed to be that the task-switching penalty was essentially zero. We see this as companies everywhere assign knowledge workers in fragments, sometimes with as many as eight or ten different tasks allocated to a single person. The prevalence of this practice amounts to a frequently repeated assertion that there is *no penalty* or that it is so minor as to be ignorable.

Even without further proof of which of these two assertions is more likely to be correct, 0 percent or 15 percent, I hope you would feel at least a little bit uncomfortable with the 0 percent premise. As it turns out, though, I have some evidence that is stronger than repeated assertion. Starting in 1984, my colleagues and I at the Atlantic Systems Guild began a three-year empirical study of software developers.[1] We enticed some six

---

[1] One of the study's published reports was "Programmer Performance and the Effects of the Workplace," *Proceedings of the 8th International Conference on Software Engineering* (London: IEEE Computer Society Press, 1985).

hundred programmers from more than a hundred organizations to test their skills against a benchmark of software development tasks. Participants worked in their own space, using their own facilities. They were also subjected to the normal run of interrupts, task switches, and ambient noise. We collected information about the environment and recorded each and every task switch. To no one's surprise, people who were interrupted less often performed better. We modeled performance against task-switching frequency and came to the conclusion that the best way to understand task switching was to assume that each switch imposes a direct penalty of a bit more than twenty minutes of lost concentration. We also noted an average of nearly 0.4 switches per hour. This results in a direct loss of productive effort of more than one hour per day.

What the Penalty Implies

A mainstay of corporate restructuring in the past decade has been to get rid of people and share their work among those remaining. This has drastically increased fragmentation of workers. Such a restructuring tactic only makes sense if the task-switching penalty is smaller than the potential savings. In practice, it only makes sense if the penalty is essentially zero. But it never is.

To the extent that a hidden task-switching penalty is now using up the resources of an overfragmented organization, the savings have been illusory. Fragmented knowledge workers may look busy, but a lot of their busyness is just thrashing, switching continually from one activity to another.

To make matters worse, the decision about who should go and who should stay was usually based on proven performance. But work performance is not an abstraction: You can't say that Ted is a high-performance worker in general, only that he has proved himself good at doing some one particular thing. Fragmentation will result in his doing less of that thing and more of something else, something he probably isn't so good at. Even without the task-switching penalty, his performance is worsened.

Knowledge workers aren't fungible. Treating them as if they were will increase busyness but make it harder for them to get useful work done.

4

When "Hurry Up" Really Means "Slow Down"

THE STORY SO FAR: Organizations sometimes become obsessed with efficiency and make themselves so busy that responsiveness and net effectiveness suffer. When this happens, it is almost always the result of a restructuring or corporate "improvement" effort gone wrong. For this reason, I refer to such an organization as *overimproved*.

The Hurry Up Mantra

Judging from the stories you hear about how busy everyone is these days, you might conclude that there are a lot of overimproved organizations out there. In the course of a normal year, I find myself visiting a dozen or more companies, agencies, and nonprofits, and working with employees of several hundred others at seminars and conferences. From my visits and from anecdotal evidence collected from seminar attendees and colleagues, I conclude that a third to a half of the organizations represented are overimproved to some extent. That is, their people are pathologically busy, frantic, and at least a little bit fearful.

In such an organization, there is a characteristic mantra that goes something like this: "Hurry up, hurry up, hurry up, hurry up, hurry up . . ." I admit, there was a time during my novice years as a manager when I was gratified by this mantra. It made me feel that I was having impact. Today I think of that mantra as the sound of an organization going wrong.

How We Work Together

I am concerned about the cases when Hurry Up really means Slow Down. To understand this possibility, it helps to return to the model of the organization as a linked set of tasks where the nodes are people and the links are passed information, work products, and by-products.

Any natural unevenness in the tasks will cause some ineffi-ciency: for example, Elaine remaining idle while she awaits input from Harry. The overimproved variant of the same oper-ation increases efficiency (or at least busyness) by reducing manpower at each of the nodes—we assign some of the workers part-time to other tasks—until the system runs with buffers, never building up too much and never emptying. Now everyone is 100 percent busy all the time.

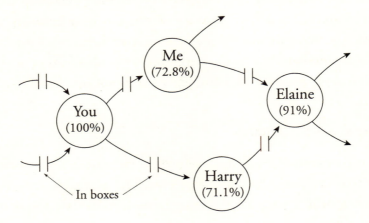

As a static picture this may look efficient. But in modern knowledge work, nothing is ever static. Things change on a day-to-day basis. This results in new unevenness of the tasks, with some people incurring additional work (their buffers build up), while others become less well loaded, since someone ahead of them in the work chain is slower to generate their particular kind of work to pass along.

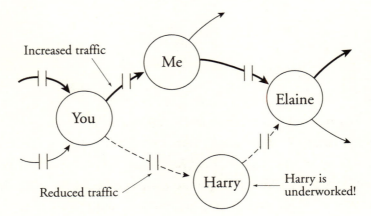

Now put yourself in Harry's place when this happens. He notes that his buffer is emptying. He also notes the pervasive mantra of Hurry Up, Hurry Up, which he interprets to mean Stay Busy. With everyone around him working furiously, he is never going to feel safe if he finishes the last item in his in-box and then waits patiently for someone to feed him something else to work on. You can understand why he might conclude that his job security is not well served by his appearing to be idle.

The survival tactic that Harry and others like him hit upon when their buffers begin to empty is to *slow down*. He slows down only enough to keep his supply of waiting work stable. If he slowed down more than that, he would appear to be a bottleneck, which would focus management on his work rate. So he doesn't do that; he slows down just enough. Harry is now busy 100 percent of the time, has a healthy buffer of work waiting for him, and is not a bottleneck. This *is* a recipe for job security; the guy is obviously an ideal employee, judged by his part in helping the Hurry Up organization to work smoothly.

That's how the Hurry Up mantra and an increased focus on busyness can end up causing people to slow down. If that's what you want, go for it.

5

Managing Eve

IN SPITE of years of parochial schooling, I have come away with a view of the creation story that differs somewhat from what the nuns must have hoped. In my view, the great heroic figure of the story is Eve. She is everything that I respect in a person: irrepressibly curious, courageous, undaunted by authority. Most of all, she is intent upon personal growth, determined to fulfill not just some but *all* of her promise.

Remember the story of her "fall." She was told that she might eat of everything in the garden except one thing: She could not eat of the Tree of Knowledge of Good and Evil. The fruit of this tree was not food at all, but understanding. If she ate it, she would know things that she was not intended to know, hence the proscription.

Eve's response to this rule was, essentially, "No way, José." She was not about to allow her growth as a person to be so limited. She ate the fruit and took the consequences. I hope that I would have been so brave in her place.

Eve Working for You

If you are a great manager, then I have a hunch you've got one or more Eves working for you. She and those like her are at least part of the reason for your success. These are the people who form the heart and soul of effective organizations. But how on earth do you manage them?

Certainly not by pulling rank. You can't tell Eve to do something because you are the boss and you say it has to be done. You can't tell her that, because she doesn't give a hoot for rank. You can't impose on her goals that don't make sense to her. If you say, "Get this project done by the end of the day today *and* also fill out your Skills Inventory Census," she will look at you like you've gone bonkers. She'll do the project, because that seems important to her, and the Skills Inventory will end up in the wastebasket. If you burden her with enough tasks that seem pointless to her, she will soon be gone.

Most of all, you can't structure her work in a way that gives her no opportunity for growth. Growth is essential to Eve, as essential as her paycheck. You can no more expect her to work without meaningful challenge than you could expect her to work without salary.

The nearly equal status of challenge and pay is unique to knowledge workers. They are different from the blue-collar workers that our fathers managed a generation ago. The easy, dumb error of managing knowledge workers is to forget that they are different and assume that basic rules developed on factory floors a century ago apply to them.

The Nonprofit Model

I had occasion recently to manage a small not-for-profit organization where most of the work was done by volunteers. I noticed from the start that there was almost no way to control the work that these people did. If you looked over their shoulders enough or imposed standards that were different from their own, they would shrug and walk away from the work, leaving you to do it yourself. Control, as they see it, is their payment for working. Deny the control or assume it yourself and they're gone.

That doesn't mean you can't control the quality of their product, only that you can't *seem* to be controlling it. You have to impose your standard without seeming to do so, somehow causing it to become their standard. This is a troubling task for many managers, one that often causes them to flee the not-for-profit world and go back to the familiar for-profit organization where people do as they're told.

But people never really "do as they're told." The difference between for-profit and volunteer organizations is that in the for-profit world people do get paid and so they are willing to give up some control to the boss, to accept at least some direction. But they don't give up all control. You couldn't pay them enough for that.

This was a great revelation to me as a manager. Without ever coming to grips with how much control workers were willing to give up to their manager, I had always assumed that I nonetheless had it all; that it was my job to control everything and their job to do everything. It took me a long time to see otherwise.

Control of Information

On a recent consulting assignment, I met with a group of process improvement researchers who'd been taking surveys among management staff. They concluded that many of these managers were spending as much as 80 percent of their time in meetings. They asked me if I didn't think that was excessive. I replied that 80 percent of a manager's time might reasonably be spent with his/her workers. However, it seemed a shame to me that these managers thought of that time as meetings; I'd rather they were spending their time one-on-one with their people, or in get-togethers that were so ad hoc as to belie the description "meeting." In some confusion, the surveyors told me that the managers were spending that 80 percent of their time in meetings with people *other than their own workers*. Whatever time they spent with their own people had to come out of the remaining 20 percent.

This is a considerably different picture (and not a pretty one). What on earth could be going on during 80 percent of those managers' days? I'm afraid I know. The managers' time is spent in meeting with clients, project stakeholders, and other external entities, all the various parties to the work who are not direct reports. And then they are shuttling what they learn from these partner organizations down to the people below them on the org chart.

The premise here is that the hierarchy lines on the chart are also the only communication conduit. Information can flow only along the lines. But this is a disaster. The hierarchy lines are paths of authority. They are far too narrowband for all the information that needs to be communicated. Communication in healthy companies takes place in the white space.

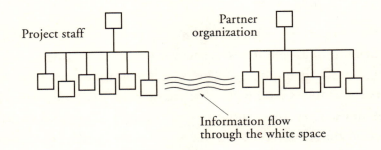

Information flow
through the white space

When communication happens *only* over the hierarchy lines, that's a priori evidence that the managers are trying to hold on to *all* control. This is not only inefficient but an insult to the people underneath. An Eve would never work for such a manager.

Control and Personal Growth

If you buy the notion that Eve is motivated largely by her craving for personal growth, then you'll understand why she cannot allow herself to be too closely controlled. She will see control as her main growth opportunity. That doesn't mean you can't control her somewhat, only that you can't control her completely. You have to give her some leeway, some opportunity to choose her own directions and make her own mistakes. Mistakes are important here. If she has control over her choices only to the extent that she makes the same ones that you would have made for her, she has no control at all. And of course she'll know that. There is no fooling Eve.

This question of control comes up primarily in choice of methods to get work done. As designer of the organization under you, you may believe that it is your responsibility to select how each task should be undertaken. Should the financials be presented in a simple spreadsheet or a simulation model? You decide on a spreadsheet. Should working designs and test plans be maintained on the Intranet or circulated on paper? You decide Intranet. Should there be a peer review of each and every work product? You decide yes.

But now suppose that Eve and her teammates decide otherwise. Don't expect for a moment that the authority vested in you by the powers-that-be will be enough to impose your way. These people are in it for growth, and the choices you're making don't allow them to grow. That's why they're looking to approach the work in a different way.

If you have built up any reserve of trust, you may be able to cash a bit of that in to get your way on some key matters. But not all. And the reserve of trust is quickly used up if you dip into it too often.

I offer the following model for control-sharing. If control is in some sense like salary, then control-sharing ought to be (or at least seem to be) proportional to salary. If you have ten people working for you and you make 25 percent more than each of them, then you get 125 "control points," and they get 100 each. If control is exercised in those proportions—or seems to be—then Eve and all her colleagues will feel that their opportunities for growth are maximized. The trick is how to assure your own requirements of the organization with just those 125 control points. That is not a trivial task. (But then, whoever said that management was easy?)

Slack in Another Sense

So here's the paradox of managing Eve: In order to keep control, you have to give it up. You have to use your authority so sparingly that no one notices that it's being used. You have to create a real sense that control is not completely centralized in your hands, but spread generously over the whole of your organization. Like a gifted helmsman, who knows that all use of the rudder increases drag and thus holds the vessel back, you have to steer with the lightest possible touch.

The slack that you thus cut for Eve and her coworkers is not slack in the time sense. This is control slack. But it is every bit as essential to the healthy organization.

6

Business Instead of Busyness

In which the author cuts to the chase and describes
the benefits of sensibly designed-in slack

THIS BOOK is divided about half and half between prescriptive and proscriptive material; half do's and half don'ts. By time-honored convention, most of the don'ts come first.

Since the early going is somewhat don't-intensive, I interrupt the plan with this chapter to give you a glimpse of what the results are likely to be if you do all or most of the do's and don't do many of the don'ts.

Brave New World

Suppose you avoided all the pitfalls discussed so far as well as the ones in the chapters just ahead. Suppose you built an organization that made explicit provision for slack, both time slack and control slack. You've tuned it up for responsiveness rather than busyness. Your people have a bit of time on their hands, time when they're not overwhelmed with work. And you're not a control freak, which leaves the Eves of your organization free to make some decisions (even some mistakes) of their own. All of that costs you something. How will it pay you back?

My short list of the benefits that come with sensibly designed-in slack includes all of the following:

- ❑ Flexibility, a capacity for ongoing organizational redesign
- ❑ Better people retention
- ❑ A capacity to invest

In the short term, these are the secondary benefits. The primary one is better responsiveness. But from the standpoint of an organization's agility in the face of changing circumstances, these three are essential. In the sections below, I comment on all three, beginning with flexibility.

An Organization in Continuing Flux

As you read these words, there is probably at least one upper manager, and possibly several, in your organization waxing enthusiastically about the importance of being able to change. They describe change as challenge, as the measure of *real* players. They talk up flexibility as a kind of Holy Grail. They exhort their underlings to strive for ultimate and total responsiveness to changing circumstances. Embrace change, they intone, adapt, accommodate, adjust. When the boss is done with the pep talk, people go back to work.

Yes, an ability to change is essential. Like many good things, it costs money. How much should it cost? Only the time and energy of a substantial portion of the people who are now 100 percent busy doing work.

Change represents investment. You invest in a change by paying for its two key components: conceptualization (or design) and implementation. This is work that can't usually be done by an elite corps of change specialists; it needs to be done by the very people who are to be changed. The reason for this is not too complex: Change is not an ad hoc business—organizational death is right around the corner if change happens only when the change specialists get around to it. Ability to change has to be an organic part of the organization. Change has to be going on all the time, everywhere. It needs to be everybody's business.

That means that everybody needs to have some capacity to devote to change. This is time that people dedicate to rethinking how their piece of the whole works, and how it ought to work. Once the change is under way, more time is required to practice new ways and to master new skills. That's the cost. The benefit is vitality and a firm grip on the future.

Slack is the way you invest in change. Slack represents operational capacity sacrificed in the interests of long-term health.

Human Capital

Healthy knowledge companies keep their people. Sure, you already know it's important to keep your *best* people. There is no question that losing one or more of these key players could jeopardize a whole project or an entire reporting period's results.

From listening to managers discuss the importance of people retention, I come away with an uneasy sense that many of these managers look at the entire matter as an exercise in keeping their stars happy. But it's not only the stars that matter. Everybody matters. That's not to say that everybody is competent, that nobody ever ought to be reassigned or fired or encouraged to look elsewhere. What I do mean to say is that each time someone quits on his/her own schedule, the organization suffers a loss.

When I made the point earlier that knowledge workers aren't fungible, I stressed that they don't divide up well, that they aren't easily able to cover different kinds of tasks, switching back and forth from day to day or hour to hour. Part of the reason for this is that one core capability that a knowledge worker brings to the task is *domain knowledge*. Whether this person is a designer, product manager, programmer, writer, consultant, or whatever, he/she comes with (1) a set of skills and (2) some explicit knowledge of the area in which skills are to be deployed. The skills alone aren't enough. Domain knowledge is also required.

The more important that domain knowledge is, the less fungible the people are. That means you can't divide them up into pieces, but it also means that you can't easily replace them with other people when they leave.

The right way to think about domain knowledge is as a corporate capital asset, as dollars of investment in the head of each knowledge worker, put there by organizational investment in that employee. When that person leaves, the asset is gone. If you did a rigorous accounting of this *human capital,* you would be obliged to declare an extraordinary loss each time one of your people quit.

How Much Is Human Capital Worth?

It's worth going through the exercise to quantify the human capital represented by the people who work for you. Think of an average performer in your group. I'm going to call him Orin. We could assess the value of Orin's domain knowledge by following him around over the years as he acquired it and charging the learning part of his salary and overhead to capital (the rest would be treated as expense).

Rather than go through this laborious exercise, let's approximate with a trick: Assume that Orin is about to leave. He waltzes in one day and informs you that he will be gone at the end of the month. His job doesn't go away, so you scurry about to hire a replacement. Let's say the replacement's name is Oliver. Oliver arrives the day after Orin departs. I think you will agree that Oliver is essentially useless on his first day, since most of what he's doing is getting his bearings (this, too, is part of the acquisition of domain knowledge). He's even worse than useless, as he is using up other people's time to get him jump-started.

On some day in the future, you will conclude that Oliver has learned enough to be essentially as useful as Orin was. How long this takes is a function of how unique your domain is, and how different it is from the last place that Oliver worked. If you're the pension accounting group of a plain-vanilla insurance company, and your Oliver last worked for one of your competitors doing almost the exact same work in the same context, then he will probably be completely up to speed in a month. If you're a telecommunications company that makes specialty packet sniffers, like one of my clients, and Oliver has only a general background in communications protocols, he may take as much as two years to be able to carry as much weight as Orin was carrying before he left. Write down your best guess of how long it will take Oliver to become the total equivalent of Orin. Express the result in months. My approximation for the value of the investment in Oliver is:

Human Capital = Time to get up to speed × (Salary + Overhead) × 50%

Oliver is 0 percent useful on the first day of this period and 100 percent useful on the last day, so I have made a simple straight-line assumption about his improving usefulness over the period. Thus, if it takes him six months to get up to speed, then your investment in his domain knowledge is 50 percent of that, or three times his total monthly cost.

Viewed another way, when Orin left, your capital loss was, similarly, three person-months.

Aggregate Human Capital and Capital Drain

Assume for a moment that all your people have a human capital invested in them similar to Orin's. Multiply the capital write-down for the loss of an Orin by number of Orins. This is your aggregate human capital.

Example:

Knowledge-worker staff	30 people
Average ramp-up time	6 months
Average cost per person-month (plus overhead)	$7,500
Aggregate human capital (30 × 6 × $7,500 × 50%)	$675,000

Similarly, you could calculate the rate at which this capital asset is draining out of your organization due to the loss of people. Multiply the frequency of personnel turnover that you've been experiencing recently by the human capital of one person.

$$\text{Human Capital Drain} = \text{Loss}_{Orin} \times \% \text{ staff turnover per month}$$

For a turnover of 24 percent (2 percent per month), the drain is $13,500 per month. If it takes a full year rather than half a year to bring an Orin up to speed, then the drain due to turnover is twice as high, or $27,000 per month. This comes to 12 percent of your entire manpower budget (30 × $7,500).

Twelve percent of your entire productive capacity is burned up replacing lost human capital. None of that effort is available to do any useful work. As you can see, ongoing human capital drain can be a substantial burden on your ability to get work done.

The analysis so far is of an organization in relative stasis. If things are changing, the human capital loss is worse. Whenever you act to change an organization, the cost of the change ends up as increased human capital in the heads of the people who implement the change. During the change, each person who drifts away costs you as much as double what such a loss would be in the steady state.

Before getting to the relationship between slack and turnover, I need to mention the special case of organizations doing project work. On projects, the turnover calculus works somewhat differently. First of all, the extent of required domain knowledge is larger, since there are two important domains to master: the business area being impacted by the project, and the project itself (its technology, for example). Further, since projects have a finite end in the not-too-distant future, untimely loss of project personnel can be still more injurious to the effort: The entire human capital replacement cost of someone who quits has to be borne by the project even though the ramp-up time may extend out beyond the project end. It might make perfect sense from the viewpoint of the organization as a whole to replace an Orin when he leaves near the end of your project, but it might not make sense from the project's point of view. You as project manager may realize that you could finish earlier by limping along to the end with no one in Orin's place. The burden of bringing an Oliver up to speed may not be paid back in the short period between his arrival and project end.

All of this explains why the loss of even nonstar performers can be a serious burden on effectiveness. Companies within a single industry often have variations of turnover rate of as much as three or four times. Those with the higher turnovers are laboring under a huge penalty. But what can they do about it?

Stanching the Flow

The reasons that people leave or don't leave are as various as the people themselves. However, a common feature of exit interviews is a sense that the departing person felt *used*. This leads to a disturbing paradox: The more successful a company is in extracting every bit of capacity from its workers, the more it exposes itself to turnover and attendant human capital loss.

On the other hand, when people stay on, they are often motivated by the lure of personal growth. The organization's agility, its healthy capability to take on change, is an important factor in supplying opportunities for such growth to the individual.

Of course, other things matter as well. Managers who inspire extraordinary loyalty from their people tend to be highly charismatic, humorous, good-looking, and tall. So, by all means, strive to be those things. If you don't feel able to improve any of those factors very much, you might consider holding on to your people by designing a little slack into their lives.

The Organization's Capacity to Invest in Itself

So far I have talked about two kinds of investment: the cost of change and the human capital represented by domain knowledge. Neither of these is usually treated as investment in conventional accounting practice, so even if my use of the i-word is justifiable, it is strictly nonstandard. What most people think of as investment is transfer of cash or liquid assets into some less liquid capital asset that the accountants are comfortable treating as investment. So, for example, your company invests when it uses cash on hand or incurs debt in order to build a new headquarters building. It invests when it buys another company or expands into a new territory or gears up for a new product line.

In my terms, you're investing in yourself when you extend or enlarge your presence in a market that is already partly yours. And you're investing in someone else when you buy your way into a market where you had no presence before and no in-house capacity to build one. A few examples: Microsoft was investing in itself when it built Windows-NT; Ford was investing in itself when it acquired Volvo; Beatrice Foods was investing in someone else when it bought Morgan Yachts; IBM was investing in someone else when it bought Lotus.

It makes a lot of sense to invest in someone else when you have already saturated or nearly saturated your market. This is something that G.E. and Disney, to take two very successful examples, do all the time. For many large corporations, this kind of outside investment is the special role of the CEO. I'm not knocking it. I am much more concerned, though, when smaller companies invest outside their own product areas. I see this as bankruptcy of inventiveness. It is particularly evident when companies find themselves with extra leverage due to run-up of their stock price. Their willingness to spend this found capital outside their own backyard is a signal that they have no real vision, no idea of how to grow in the arena that they know best.

What I call bankruptcy of inventiveness is often the result of a failure to set aside the resources necessary to let invention happen. The principal resource needed for invention is slack.

When companies can't invent, it's usually because their people are too damn busy.

A Penny Saved . . .

People who are charged with making a company more efficient by removing slack justify what they're doing by talking about bottom-line benefit. A penny saved, they reason, is a penny earned. They know that's true because they've heard it said so many times. With some trepidation, I now enter into direct conflict with the wisdom of the ages to suggest that

A penny saved is *not* a penny earned.

At least not all pennies saved. Cutting money out of this year's expenditure for the company yacht might go directly to the bottom line, but cutting from R&D is something else entirely. Because the R&D expenditure is investment, trimming it may succeed only in moving profit from next year's bottom line to this year's. It may add to this year's net but reduce the profit stream for next year and many years after. The present value of the future revenue stream is almost always much greater than the cost this year—that's why you invest in R&D. A penny saved from any kind of investment is never a penny earned.

Slack is a kind of investment. Learning to think of it that way (instead of as waste) is what distinguishes organizations that are "in business" from those that are merely busy.

Part Two

Lost, but Making Good Time

At a computer conference in Austin, Texas, a few years back, I happened to bump into my friend and colleague Capers Jones in the hotel lobby. We sought out a pair of overstuffed chairs and gave ourselves the luxury of an hour to catch up on each other's recent doings and to shoot the breeze. Capers is the founder of a now-prestigious company that specializes in scheduling and estimation of complex development projects. The company makes a sophisticated line of parametric analysis tools. Capers pulled out a laptop and, right there in the hotel lobby, gave me a spiffy demo of the most recent version. The tool asks you a series of questions about your project and then proposes likely schedules, manpower loading patterns, interim deliverables, and the like. In the query stage, the package asks for guidance about what to optimize. You are presented with a pair of radio buttons:

❑ Minimize time
❑ Minimize cost

You have to pick one or the other.

"My clients give me a lot of grief about this choice," Capers told me. "They tell me that what they really want to do is minimize *both* time and cost."

Capers patiently explains to them the impossibility of minimizing both of two mutually dependent variables. You can minimize some weighted combination of the two, he tells them, but it doesn't make sense to . . . By this time, their eyes would be glazing over.

"I'm half tempted," he told me, "to put in a third radio button for 'Minimize *both* time and cost.' It's a logical absurdity, of course, but they seem to need it. Then the tool would have to make some reasonable assumption about the relative weighting of the two."

The need for that third radio button tells us something more than a little bit sad about modern-day management: Managers in all parts of our economy are under enormous pressure to do everything much faster and much more cheaply, to minimize *both* time and cost. Logically absurd or not, that is the charter given to them, and they've got to work with it.

When you're torn between two mutually exclusive goals, when there is no room for give in either one, the result is stress. Managers everywhere are under stress, and stress, as we all know, is bad for the health, tough on relationships, and causes poor judgment. That's the effect of stress on the individual. What's less well appreciated is the effect of stress on organizations. In the following chapters, I examine some of the symptoms and behaviors of overstressed organizations. Among those symptoms and behaviors are declining health, failing relationships (with customers and employees), and a lot of lousy judgment.

When stress is the problem, slack is the solution. From this perspective, organizational stress looks like nothing more than a sign of deficient slack. For want of needed slack, organizations become frenzied, fearful, and risk averse, and their key employees wander away, looking for someplace more sensible to work.

7

The Cost of Pressure

THE HURRY UP ORGANIZATION is under constant pressure. You, in your role as manager, certainly contribute to this pressure, either consciously or unconsciously. After all, you are under a lot of pressure yourself, so why not pass it down to the people below you on the hierarchy? Similarly, to the extent that you show yourself to be accepting of pressure and able to thrive on it, you're applying more pressure on your peer managers as well. They can't let themselves be perceived as less up for the challenge than you are.

You apply pressure to your subordinates in a number of different ways, some of them obvious and some not. You do this, for example, by

❑ Turning the screws on delivery dates (aggressive scheduling)
❑ Loading on extra work
❑ Encouraging overtime
❑ Getting angry when disappointed

❏ Noting one subordinate's extraordinary effort and prais-
ing it in the presence of the others

❏ Being severe about anything other than superb performance

❏ Expecting great things of all your workers

❏ Railing against any apparent waste of time

❏ Setting an example yourself (with the boss laboring so
mightily, there is certainly no time for anybody else to
goof off)

❏ Creating incentives to encourage desired behavior or results

Incentives for knowledge workers are, to my mind, a sad indicator of management that just doesn't know how to manage.
First of all, the incentives are usually dinky: Meet a deadline
and everybody on the team gets 5,000 Advantage Miles, re-
deemable for travel and other goodies. Yawn. It would be different if the prize were a few million bucks to be divided up
among the six people who brought the project home ahead of
schedule. It's intriguing to think how that might encourage
out-of-the-box thinking to achieve an end. But Advantage
Miles? A plaque? A Certificate of Appreciation? Empty honors
like Employee of the Month or Team of the Month? Get serious.

Such incentives don't really encourage any kind of different behavior in the people they target. But they do increase
pressure by sending a loud and clear message that management wants everybody to get cracking. But wait a minute. How
can they increase pressure without changing behavior? Pressure up and behavior unchanged? Is that even possible? It is.
That's my point. Most of the things you do to increase pressure
don't change people's behavior in any meaningful way.

This assertion certainly wouldn't have passed muster with me during most of my life as a manager, so I hardly expect you to swallow it whole. But please read on . . .

A Model of Pressure and Its Effect

Instead of all the indirect and subtle ways you have to apply pressure, imagine you had a very direct and unsubtle one: a huge lever beside your desk. When you push the lever down, pressure is increased on all your people. When you pull it back, pressure is reduced. Push the lever all the way down and the pressure is at its maximum. Now, what's your tactic for use of the lever?

As you consider moving the lever one way or another, I have a hunch that there is a tiny voice somewhere inside your head telling you to push the damn thing all the way down to the floor and leave it there forever. This is not, strictly speaking, *your* voice. Rather, it is the corporate culture speaking through you. An increasingly common bit of our organizational folklore holds that pressure improves performance and that maximum performance can occur only in the presence of maximum pressure. This idea, though deeply embedded in our culture, doesn't stand up to examination in the light of day.

In order to cast some light on the matter, I offer the following gedanken experiment: Suppose you could know that a given project would take your team of three workers exactly twelve months to complete in a total absence of pressure. In this scenario, you give the workers no incentive beyond "Let me know when you're done." And they're done in twelve months.

Now further suppose that you have on hand a number of absolutely identically skilled teams who know nothing of each other's existence. You subsequently assign the same task to a number of these, varying the amount of pressure for each experiment. You note the position of the pressure lever and correlate it to performance (elapsed months to complete the work). When you've run, say, a hundred trials, you plot the result into a Pressure vs. Elapsed Time graph of the form shown below. Each point on the graph represents one performance of the work. Initially, you have only one.

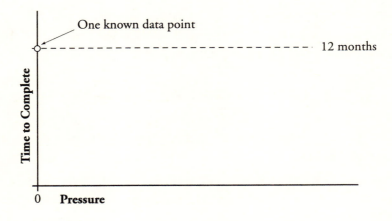

The effect of pressure on time to complete

Before you read on, I encourage you to commit yourself as to what the graph will look like when you add the other 99 points. What shape will it take on? Will elapsed time be reduced as pressure is applied? If so, by how much? Are the potential savings of time limited? (I haven't told you too much about the actual work to be done, but remember that it is knowledge work.) Will it be possible to reduce elapsed time by 25 percent or more through the use of pressure? Fifty percent? Once you've determined the lever setting that produces minimum elapsed time, what will be the result of pushing it down still more? Is it possible to apply too much pressure? Is it possible to apply enough pressure to result in the work taking longer than twelve months?

Before I show you my own answer, let's take a look at what seems to be the graph implied by current folklore. I offer this without any endorsement; in fact, I think it is wrong, wrong, dead wrong. But here it is:

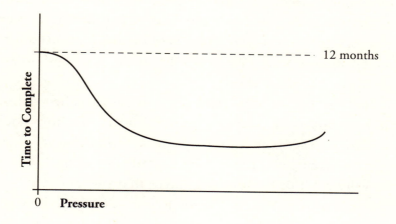

Wrong, wrong, dead wrong

In this view, pressure seems to have a huge effect: It can reduce elapsed time by 50 percent or more. If people under no pressure at all can do the work in twelve months, this model suggests that the same people under sufficient pressure might be able to do the same work in five. Increasing pressure beyond this point has no beneficial effect, since people are already proceeding at maximum speed. But it does no harm either. The curve is essentially flat beyond the minimum elapsed time point. That's handy, since it's hard to know exactly how much pressure is best; the model counsels you to err on the side of too much pressure.

As a concession to the nutsy granola types, the model grudgingly acknowledges that a *truly excessive* amount of pressure (the extreme right-hand side of the graph) might actually cause performance decrease. If you are completely unreasonable, it's possible that people will rebel and begin to slow down.

Lister's Law

If your workers were galley slaves and your lever were a whip, you might expect that applying the whip would make them pick up the work pace. More whipping makes them row faster until they just can't row any faster because they are maxed out. The pressure vs. work rate model shown above is more or less confirmed, for galley slaves at least.

But the people who work for you aren't galley slaves. They are knowledge workers. I am about to reveal to you an astounding fact about knowledge workers and how they are different from galley slaves. The second you digest this fact, you will find it difficult to remember that you didn't always know it was true. You will persuade yourself that you always knew it. (But if you always knew it, you might wonder why you have been prone to use pressure the way you have.) The astounding fact comes from my friend and colleague Tim Lister.

> "People under time pressure don't *think* faster."
> —Tim Lister

Think rate is fixed. No matter what you do, no matter how hard you try, you can't pick up the pace of thinking.

Lister's astounding fact tells us that the galley slave model is entirely wrong for knowledge workers. Since they can't alter the rate of mental discriminations (basic elements of knowledge work) per second, their potential to respond to pressure is severely limited. All they can do is

❑ Eliminate wasted time
❑ Defer tasks that are not on the critical path
❑ Stay late

Well, you might think, it's too bad they can't pick up the work pace, but given that they can't, the three ways they tend to respond to pressure all sound constructive. Who could argue, for example, against routing out waste? And I would agree. But while the direction of these actions may be correct, the magnitude is limited. In a healthy knowledge-worker organization, people don't waste a lot of time anyway, since wasted time is an affront to them as much as it is to their management. They are more likely to be frustrated by wasted time than enjoy it. If they aren't wasting much time even in the no-pressure situation, they won't make much improvement when the pressure increases. Similarly, people aren't inclined to work on tasks in the wrong order, since they derive satisfaction from accomplishment, and a motivation toward meaningful accomplishment tends to steer them onto the critical path. A little pressure might decrease wasted time slightly and cause an equally slight improvement in focusing on the critical path.

Staying late is quite another matter. In the short term, it can certainly have an impressive effect: A worker might stay one day until midnight, for example, and actually accomplish twice as much in this extended day as he/she would have accomplished in a normal day. But the likelihood of realizing this same gain by staying late the next day and the day after is rather poor. In any event, the most dedicated worker can't put in nearly enough extra time over the course of months to get the kind of performance increase suggested by the galley slave model. There just isn't enough time in the day, and besides, the increasing pressures from family and personal life will soon tend to right the balance.

A Better Model

A more realistic model of how pressure impacts performance is, I believe, shown in the graph below.

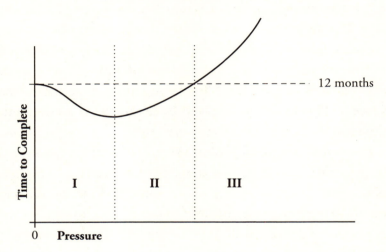

Here we see that pressure has a fairly limited capacity to reduce delivery time, maybe 10 or 15 percent at the most. And excessive pressure can quickly begin to worsen performance. The model is divided into three regions.

❑ In Region I, workers are responding to increased pressure by trimming any remaining waste, by concentrating on the critical path, and by staying late.

❑ In Region II, workers are getting tired, feeling pressure from home, and starting to put in a little "undertime" (taking the kid to the dentist during work hours, since the company owes them so much time anyway).

❑ In Region III, workers are polishing up their résumés and beginning to look for work elsewhere.

So What Does It All Mean?

Pressure is not entirely irrelevant to performance, but it is certainly not the end-all that most of us try to make of it, at least during some part of our management careers. Managers who think of pushing the lever as a major part of what management is all about are missing most of what management is all about. Yet it is not entirely their fault. They were drawn into management because they wanted to do something more gratifying than apply endless pressure on the poor souls lower down the hierarchy.

It's the stressed-out organization that elevates the use of pressure to its prominent status. It makes its managers apply far too much. The long-term effect of too much pressure is demotivation, burnout, and loss of key people. The best managers use pressure only rarely and never over extended periods.

8

Aggressive Schedules

DURING THE COURSE of a year, I visit half a dozen or more development projects going on at major corporations around the world. All of these endeavors are under pressure to deliver their products as soon as possible, but some of them are more stressed than others. In the most highly stressed projects, people at all levels talk about the schedule being "aggressive," or even "highly aggressive." In my experience, projects in which the schedule is commonly termed aggressive or highly aggressive invariably turn out to be fiascoes. "Aggressive schedule," I've come to suspect, is a kind of code phrase—understood implicitly by all involved—for a schedule that is absurd, that has no chance at all of being met.

The key here is that the schedule be *patently* absurd; just not *demonstrably* absurd. And sure enough, the actual project will end up a year or two years late—or even worse, be canceled a year or two years after the original delivery date. Now whenever I hear the words "aggressive schedule," I think of heading for the exit.

The Overcommitment Ethic

How do we managers ever get ourselves in the position of signing on to these "aggressive" dates? Could it be that in the commitment stage of project work something comes over us the way the evil Mr. Hyde could take over kindly Dr. Jekyll? We take an already risky endeavor and complicate it further by making or signing on to commitments that are at or beyond the hairy edge of possibility.

Managers during the commitment process can be like little boys posturing before a schoolyard fight: "I'm gonna knock your block off." "I'm gonna wipe up the floor with you." "I'm gonna hit you so hard your teeth will rattle." This posturing is inconsistent with the desultory performance of the fight that follows (if there even is one), and even further removed from the demonstrated performance of fights past. So, too, the over-committing manager. He/she promises a level of performance not achieved in the past and not likely to be achieved in the future.

Overcommitment is not just an accident. Companies sometimes take purposeful steps to build an overcommitment ethic into their managers and into the corporate culture. I recently visited an off-site training experience where a hundred or so professional project managers were subjected to one whole evening of Formula One race videos, complete with the requisite number of clips showing horrible crashes and near-death experiences. Formula One is a sport in which participants risk their lives to push the envelope of performance by tiny increments. There is no prize for finishing second. What message was the company sending by showing its managers these videos? The clear implication was that it wanted its managers to go for broke. Small wonder, then, that so many of the projects they manage do in fact end up broke.

Article of Faith

Encouraging overcommitment may seem bizarre to someone on the outside. That's because an outsider is not familiar with an article of faith common to many managers and project personnel: the idea that starting any endeavor out with a highly aggressive (i.e., impossible) delivery date may not actually achieve the date, but at least won't do the effort any harm. So, for example, if you set out to bring a project to completion in twelve months, and it actually takes you eighteen, you console yourself by saying, "Thank goodness we started out fast. Otherwise we might still be working on the stupid thing."

I've called this idea an article of faith. Like religious articles of faith, it is a premise that the believer is obliged to accept without question. In fact, there may even be an element of sin associated with doubt. To a nonbeliever, the premise looks dubious at best, but the faithful *must* believe. Project managers are taught from their earliest years that striving toward even the most impossible schedule can do no harm.

I am not a believer. The notion that impossible schedules *don't* damage projects strikes me as ludicrous. If you set out, for example, to build a two-thousand-square-foot home in one week, your colleagues may warn you that this kind of performance is not consistent with reality. You reply, as did one of my client managers, "Who's talking about reality here? We're talking about the project plan."

A quick calculation shows that if you're going to be done by Friday, you will need at least fifty skilled framers on the site and ready to swing their hammers no later than Tuesday. That means the foundation has got to be poured and (somehow) cured on Monday. When that doesn't happen, you've got fifty framers staring at you all day Tuesday, wondering what they're there for. Materials begin arriving long before they can be used and you direct the framers to off-load and store them, maybe even to build a shed where they can be protected from the weather. Plumbers show up before there is anything to plumb, and electricians are on-site but there is nothing to wire, so you direct them all to help the fifty framers build the shed. By the time you finally do finish the house, it will have cost you more and taken longer than if you'd started out with a more reasonable schedule. After it's all over, I hope you won't be inclined to delude yourself that starting off fast was a winning strategy.

Accountability

When a schedule is not met, those inclined to pass out blame are quick to point at the lowest-level workers; they reason that performance is the domain entirely of those who *perform* the work. They ask plaintively, "Why can't these guys ever meet their schedules?" The answer that the schedule might have been wrong in the first place only befuddles them. It's as though they believe there is no such thing as a bad schedule, only bad performances that resulted in missing the scheduled date.

There *is* such a thing as a bad schedule. A bad schedule is one that sets a date that is subsequently missed. That's it. That's the beginning and the end of how a schedule should be judged. If the date is missed, the schedule was wrong. It doesn't matter why the date was missed. The purpose of the schedule was planning, not goal-setting. Work that is not performed according to a plan invalidates the plan.

The missed schedule indicts the planners, not the workers. Even if the workers are utterly incompetent, a plan that takes careful note of their inadequacies can help to minimize the damage. A plan that takes no account of realities is not just useless but dangerous.

When the schedule is wrong, the work goes on anyway, proceeding in some way other than as planned. The result is that the effort is necessarily hurt. Subtasks are taken in a wrong order, or declared done when they're only half done, all to keep the fiction of the schedule alive as long as possible. When the difference between plan and actual is minor, it probably doesn't matter much. But when the difference is substantial, when, for example, a project is scheduled to come home within one year and it actually finishes in eighteen or twenty-four months, the damage attributable to the bad schedule can be huge.

The people who *set* the schedule, not just the ones who failed to meet it, need to be held accountable. The marketing manager, for example, who throws a tantrum to force a new project to commit to the one-year schedule has to accept responsibility when the project actually takes two. Forcing a project onto an unrealistic schedule is dangerous for the company and has to be made dangerous as well for those who impose the schedule.

9
Overtime

I OFFICIALLY ENTERED the workforce as a full-time employee on September 3, 1963. I showed up early that morning at Bell Telephone Laboratories' Holmdel, New Jersey, facility. My boss, Lee Toumenoksa, received me in his office and gave me the little Welcome to the World of Work lecture that he'd probably given to dozens of other just-out-of-college kids before me. The first matter he dealt with was the official workday: Work began, he told me, at 8:15 A.M. and continued until 4:45 P.M. We were expected to take an hour for lunch, so that worked out to a seven-and-a-half-hour day, a 37.5-hour week. Lee told me he was a bear about the 8:15 starting time. "Do me a favor," he said, "and don't ever come in a little bit late. If you have to be late one day for some reason, be two or three hours late, not two or three minutes late. If you're coming in 'on time,' then I expect you to be here and working by 8:15."

Before I left Lee's office that morning, I'd had one thing fairly energetically imprinted on my newly minted work ethic: I owed the Labs seven and a half hours of work every single workday. Not less and not more. This was "the deal" of my employment. Shortchanging the Labs on work hours would have been a cheat, just as much as if they shortchanged my paycheck.

Why seven and a half hours? That number was consciously designed into the structure of Bell Telephone Laboratories every bit as much as the hierarchy of management and the package of benefits were designed in. Lee and his colleagues in upper management had come to the considered opinion that seven and a half hours was the right amount of time to ask an employee to work. Less than that, they concluded, would have wasted a resource that was available to them. More would have caused the quality of work to suffer or would have made "the deal" of employment enough less attractive that fewer new employees would accept offers and more veterans would wander away to the competition.

The decision to work overtime or to encourage others to do so is to override a fundamental design decision, one of the intrinsics of the enterprise. It is to say that that decision was wrong in the first place, that seven and a half hours, for example, was simply too little. It is the assertion that altering the deal to extract ten or eleven or twelve hours per day for the same pay will be to the organization's real advantage.

This is an extremely dubious proposition. Companies the world over have standardized a work regime for knowledge workers that is on the order of seven or eight hours per day, five days a week. If you were to tinker with this by a few minutes either way—particularly if you had a good reason for doing so and some empirical evidence to back you up—I could hardly quibble. But when companies institute overtime, it's not minutes per day they're looking for. They increase the workday by huge increments, typically 40 or 50 percent. And they almost never have the courage to institutionalize this decision by redefining the official workday. I think they're kidding themselves.

Sprinting

There is a useful distinction to make here between infrequent short bursts of overtime—what I call *sprinting*—and extended overtime. Sprinting can make perfectly good sense in the right circumstances. Imagine yourself encouraging everyone to come in for a gargantuan workathon weekend to bring a project to completion for delivery Monday morning. You all stay up through the night, or catch catnaps on the carpet or on the sofa in the big boss's office. You keep each other going, check each other's work (after all, people do get tired), and keep everybody's spirits up. You guzzle coffee. You share order-in pizza or sandwiches from the all-night deli or you slip out for noodles at the Chinese place that keeps late hours. Most of all, you succeed on Monday morning, and when the crazy weekend is over, you go back to normal hours.

This is the stuff of which corporate legends are made. When you've all been through it together, and shared an important success, there is something profoundly changed about the culture of the organization. The energy is still there after the workathon weekend is long past.

The manager who makes effective use of the occasional sprint is a hero. He/she needs impeccable timing, a flawless sense of what can and can't be accomplished over a short period (there is no benefit if the delivery doesn't take place on Monday or if it gets rejected), and enough raw leadership talent to pull the whole affair together. Finally, such a manager also needs to have a huge reserve of trust to dip into, the clear sense shared by all that the call for extraordinary effort is truly extraordinary, not likely to be wasted and not likely to become a regular fixture.

Extended Overtime

Sprinting at the end of a marathon makes good sense, but sprinting through the whole twenty-six-mile race makes no sense at all. You would sprint for a few hundred yards, then roll around on the ground clutching your gut and gasping for breath for a few minutes more before you could even think of making another short sprint. The sprint-gasp-sprint-gasp marathon would probably take you twice as long to complete as a more normally run twenty-six miles.

That's pretty obvious for running, but a bit less obvious when the equivalent of sprinting is overtime. It's less obvious because knowledge workers who have just finished a short burst of sprinting (staying long into the night, for example) are obliged to cover up the gasping phase. They stay on the job, looking bleary and babbling a bit, but still there. Or they disappear unnoticed to catch forty winks in the backseats of their cars.

The "long into the night" example is perhaps too extreme. A more typical overtime regime is something like this: ten- or eleven-hour days Monday through Friday plus significant weekend time, all of it amounting to sixty-plus hours for the week. In this scheme, you may get a full night's sleep every night. It's your personal life that pays the price for the extra time given to the company. Gasping, in this example, is the increasing pressure that your personal life begins to apply: strain on the marriage, kids acting out, eventually a sense of being used. Again, corporate culture requires you to conceal the gasping, but it's there. It takes its toll in lost work hours, ineffectively spent time, reduced quality, and people tossing in the towel to search for more sensible jobs.

Yes, but is this toll less than the net positive effect of the extra hours contributed by the employee? If it were, extended overtime would be a net benefit to the organization—no matter what its cost—and the manager who extracted it from his/her people would be doing good. If only management were so simple. It isn't.

An Important Productivity-Reduction Technique

Extended overtime is a productivity-reduction technique. It reduces the effect of each hour worked. We can quantify the productivity reduction, at least broadly, by looking at certain kinds of knowledge work where there are widely accepted metrics of work accomplished.

In fields such as circuit design, architectural design, and software development, predictive metrics are widely used to project future effort based on early available indicators. So, for example, the total effort to test and prove new circuits may be correlated to the number of junctions in the circuits as follows:

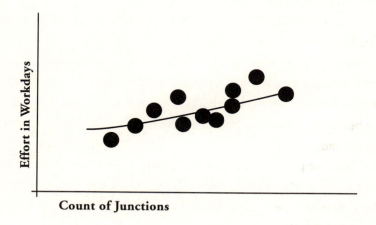

Now, to forecast what will be required to prove out a new circuit, count the number of junctions in the circuit and let the trend line indicate expected effort.

The people who design such metric relationships take particular pains to define their formulas and procedures so as to narrow the scatter of data points around the prediction line. (Obviously, the graph shown above would be less useful if the points were more widely scattered away from the line.) Any refinement of approach that narrows scatter is an improvement. One "improvement" you might think to suggest is to correlate the values of any metric to *work hours* rather than workdays, since workdays on some projects are much longer (due to overtime) than those on other projects. But surprisingly, when the researchers try out this "improvement," scatter is not reduced, it is increased. The result is that in all three of these fields, overtime is explicitly ignored in projecting effort required to perform new work. Stop and think about what that means. Some projects are working days that are 50 percent longer than others, but taking account of the variant workday does not materially reduce scatter. The only explanation is that those longer days do not accomplish more than the shorter ones. The best predictor of how much work a knowledge worker will accomplish is not the hours that he or she spends, but the days. The twelve-hour days don't accomplish any more than the eight-hour days. Overtime is a wash.

Since companies don't typically pay knowledge workers for overtime, any net advantage gained by extraction of overtime would be a cost-free benefit. That violates the ages-old adage that there ain't no such thing as a free lunch. And sure enough, there ain't.

There are four reasons why overtime hurts enough to offset the effect of the added hours. These are the invariable side effects of extended overtime:

- ❏ Reduced quality
- ❏ Personnel burnout
- ❏ Increased turnover of staff
- ❏ Ineffective use of time during normal hours

Effect on Quality

Knowledge work is, by definition, think-intensive. In any discussion of hiring new knowledge workers, we acknowledge implicitly that the quality of the candidate's thinking is all-important; that's what makes a great hire so much better than a less great one. What we are not so quick to acknowledge is what increases or decreases the quality of thinking during a day. Foremost among these is fatigue. Most knowledge workers, for example, will tell you that they really shouldn't do any kind of error-prone work late in a work session, because they know their thinking is no longer sufficiently clear for that kind of task. Very often they consider that logic and then do the error-prone task anyway (proving, I guess, that fatigue affects strategic judgment as much as tactical).

Extended overtime is not just something that companies do to their workers; workers also do it to themselves. You can't discuss the subject intelligently without taking account of the addictive, almost erotic, appeal that deep and obsessive involvement in a task can have. There is a high associated with such efforts that may cloud your judgment a bit but still feels awfully good. It makes you feel like one of the heroes of *The Right Stuff,* Tom Wolfe's marvelous recounting of the NASA space program:

> Every young fighter jock knew the feeling of getting two or three hours' sleep and then waking up at 5:30 A.M. and having a few cups of coffee, a few cigarettes, and then carting his poor quivering liver out to the field for another day of flying. There were those who arrived not merely hungover but still drunk, slapping oxygen tank cones over their faces and trying to burn the alcohol out of their systems, and then going up, remarking later: "I don't *advise* it, you understand, but it *can* be done." (Provided you have the right stuff, you miserable pudknocker.)

What's clear here is that the high, the narcotic of gonzo overindulgence, and the associated fatigue all combine to reduce the individual's mental capacities. If the quality of thinking matters, then overtime is not a great prescription.

Zombies

Overindulgence in work, like overindulgence in anything else, will eventually lead to burnout. Burned-out workers have no heart for anything—not for more overtime, not even for putting in a sensible eight hours a day. They are simply lost to the effort. If they have any capacity left at all, they will use it to conceal the burnout, or at least to try to do so. But they won't be able to do any real work. In my reviews of overstressed projects, I am constantly amazed at the presence of so many zombies on the staff, people who go through the paces but no longer contribute. And they are often the ex-stars of the enterprise.

Burned-out workers usually leave and thus fall into the turnover category, discussed below. But not always. Sometimes they stay on as zombies. Organizations with a lot of burnout begin to have a weighty, lethargic feel, just what you'd expect of a staff made up largely of the living dead.

Turnover

Because most companies don't capitalize their investment in people, they fail to note the dollar cost of their lost human capital due to turnover. They characterize their work in terms of its most important components, something like the graph at the top of the next page. When I ask the presenters, "Where is personnel turnover in this pie chart?" they look at me blankly. It isn't anywhere in the chart. Or more precisely, it is distributed over all the slices in such a way as to remain invisible.

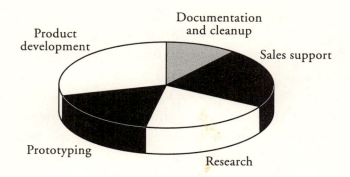

The pie charts used to show cost breakdown in your work may utilize different categories. But whatever they are, I bet turnover is not among them. That's a shame, because if it were shown explicitly, I believe it would be so large as to jar your thinking:

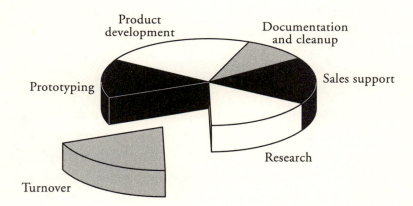

When we measure human capital carefully and use the measurements to give a cash quantification to personnel turnover, it often becomes the second or third largest cost category.

There is a substantial variation in turnover rates among companies. In comparative employment studies such as those published by the Institute of Electrical and Electronic Engineers, for example, companies whose turnover places them in the best third of the sample are experiencing less than half the turnover loss of those in the worst third.

Only by not thinking about this at all can you persist in the comfortable illusion that overtime extracted from employees will have no effect on turnover. When companies conduct exit interviews of their departing employees, overtime is a frequently cited cause of the departure. When people feel used, when the fragile balance of their lives is upset by increasing pressure on their families, they'd be crazy not to think of moving on. Many of them do. For example, in *Soul of a New Machine,* the retrospective of Data General's overtime-intensive Eagle Project, the author, Tracy Kidder, reports that every single member of the Eagle team was gone within a month of the end of the project. Even those who stayed on till the end (and many didn't) were unwilling to continue working for the kind of company that had so used them.

Wasting Time

The first three hidden costs of extended overtime are dwarfed by the fourth, a tendency to waste normal workday hours in companies that are working a lot of overtime. When people are putting in thirty or forty hours a week of overtime, the basic hygienic acts of management to reduce daytime waste are for some reason suspended.

I chided one of my clients, an engineering company in the Fortune 500, for all the overtime his people were working. "What would you do," I asked him, "if overtime were forbidden and you still had to make the schedule?" "Well, I'll tell you one thing," he answered promptly, "we'd sure have to do something about all these meetings."

I paused for a moment, hoping that the words that had

come so readily out of his mouth would make their way back in through an ear. But no. He couldn't hear what he'd just said. He missed it entirely.

Meetings were not just a problem in his organization, they were an obsession. Meetings accounted for nearly a third of all his people's time. Not only were there far too many meetings, the meetings were huge. The typical meeting I attended there had thirty or forty people present. At my initial briefing, my first day as consultant to the company, I endured a nine-hour presentation with half a dozen presenters, projectors and screens, Powerpoint slides, videos, and product demos. It was all new to me and so I got something out of the nine hours. But why on earth were there twenty-five other people present for my briefing, more than a dozen of whom never said a word? I'll tell you why: It was the kind of organization that couldn't conduct a meeting with fewer than two dozen people in a room. That was the culture.

The oversize-meeting culture was made possible only because people were putting in so many extra hours to get work done. When we trimmed overtime, the first step toward sanity was assured. They had to cut way back on meetings and trim the population of each necessary meeting back to those people who were required to make whatever decision had justified the meeting in the first place.

Meetings are only one of the ways that overtime organizations waste the time of their most essential human resources. Another is that workers tend to drop their interrupt discipline during daylight hours. Knowing that their peers will be working long into the night, they feel free to interrupt them willy-nilly during "normal" work hours. The result is that no one can get work done between nine and five, and so the tendency to work overtime is increased. The poor worker who is there at midnight has probably stayed at his or her desk after regular closing just in the hope of having some peace and quiet for a little real work. What a shame that the organization can't give such workers a decently interrupt- and noise-free environment during standard hours.

Managerial Overtime

So far I've been talking about overtime put in by knowledge workers, not their managers. But it's no secret that managers work extra hours too. If you're enticing overtime hours out of your people, you are probably obliged to stick around late into the night as much, or nearly as much, as they do. And you can't loaf during those extra hours while your people are sweating on your behalf. If you're not busy, at least you have to look busy.

When overtime is the norm for workers, their managers tend to become pure workaholics. They *run* through their days, skip lunch, and put in far too many hours. I suspect they're trying to impress someone, but not me. I'm much more impressed with a manager who never breaks a sweat, who never looks busy at all. I'm guided by a basic rule that has proved true in virtually every company I visit:

> Overworked managers are doing things they shouldn't be doing.

The main thing they are doing, the particular pathology of most overworked managers, is the subject of Chapter 12. I won't discuss it here, but will give you a clue: When managers are overworked, they're doing something other than management; the more they allow themselves to be overworked, the less real management gets done.

10

A Little Sleight of Hand in the Accounting Department

THERE IS NO LEAVING the subject of overtime without mentioning a minor case of fraud in the way we account for these extra hours in most organizations. Knowledge workers are usually not paid for overtime hours. What they are paid for is, typically, forty hours a week. A worker who has put in sixty hours in a given week now goes through a little ceremony at the end of that week, filling out some sort of a time record that reports Total Hours Worked as forty. He/she has been assured that management is well aware of the extra hours heroically contributed to the cause, but the time sheet ("really just something to keep Personnel off our backs") has to report a pro forma forty-hour week.

Productivity and Apparent Productivity

The fraud here, a kind of corporate self-deception, has to do with the way productivity is defined. Whatever work is accomplished during the week is traditionally divided by the number of hours reported, not the number of hours really worked. Workers who have been assured that their managers are deeply cognizant of their overtime hours may be unaware that the productivity figures used to measure those same managers leave out the overtime hours entirely.

This leads to an unfortunate management dynamic: Reported productivity can apparently be inflated by goading workers into working overtime; managers who extract more overtime from their workers look like more effective managers.

I say this is an apparent inflation of productivity, because the worker is almost certainly less productive during all those extra hours. So we have an approach to productivity enhancement that *leads directly to productivity reduction*. This may not be immediately evident because the work produced by knowledge workers is not easy to measure. But suppose for a moment that it were . . .

Gedankenexperiment in Productivity Measurement

Imagine that you had a magical meter that could measure actual work performed by your knowledge workers, expressed in Total Useful Mental Discriminations. Suppose it shows that a given worker produces 800 TUMD over the course of an eight-hour day. Productivity is therefore 100 TUMD per hour.

Now you somehow persuade that worker to stay an extra two hours. Your meter shows some drop-off in TUMD over the extra hours. The guy is tired and a bit distracted. He manages to achieve only 70 TUMD during hour nine and 30 TUMD during hour ten. Work accomplished during the full ten-hour day therefore total 900 TUMD. Real productivity for the day is reduced to 90 TUMD per hour (900 TUMD/10 hrs.). However, the *reported* productivity goes up:

Reported Productivity = 900 TUMD/8 hrs. = 112.5 TUMD per hour

The fiction of basing productivity measurement on hours paid rather than hours worked leads directly to "productivity improvement" schemes that make people less productive.

Particularly Pathological Variant

It gets worse. In the real world, we don't have TUMD meters. For most knowledge work, we have no objective way to measure an individual worker's meaningful output during a day. Good managers may have a keen sense of how much their people are contributing, but few can really claim to have *measured* it. In the absence of work measurement, a common technique is to assume that real work is a direct linear function of time present. This leads to a truly pathological definition of productivity:

$$\text{"Productivity"} = \frac{\text{Hours Worked}}{\text{Hours Paid}}$$

It's not uncommon for organizations to make an explicit calculation of this "productivity" and hold it up in front of managers as a performance indicator.

Yes, but in the Real World . . .

Since the company doesn't pay for the extra hours, you might argue that *its* productivity (quantity of work done per dollar of cost) does go up when people stay late, even though the people become progressively less efficient during the extra hours. Enticing our gedankenexperiment worker to stay two more hours, for example, did get the company an extra 100 TUMD, in spite of the worker's decline in real productivity. And therefore it did increase the company's total output of work by 12.5

percent at no additional cost. How can this be bad? Well, it can't, provided that you do really have a TUMD meter to confirm that total useful work per dollar paid is increased in the short run and stays at that level over the longer period. It's only in the intermediate to long term that the negative effects of overtime show up.

When people put in lots of overtime over an extended period of time, their net effectiveness is not just decreased during the extra hours; they begin to limp during the main body of the workday as well, due to built-up fatigue and reduced motivation. That can lead to less total work accomplished in a twelve-hour day than would have been accomplished in an eight-hour day. I made that point in Chapter 9. My additional point here is that the perverse definition of productivity based on the fiction of ignored overtime hours can only increase the likelihood of lowered performance.

11

Power Sweeper

MY WIFE, SALLY, and I were sitting in a pleasant little outdoor café near the water in Hilton Head, South Carolina. In the middle of our luncheon, conversations at all tables had to grind to a stop as a maintenance worker approached with his leaf sweeper roaring. Opposite me, Sally was looking less than pleased. I used one of those all-purpose male shrugs to convey that the fellow would soon be gone. Five minutes later he turned the blower off and disappeared.

"Stupid blowers," Sally muttered in the new silence.

"Oh well," I said, "it is a laborsaving device, I suppose."

She gave me one of those don't-guys-ever-see-anything-except-the-obvious? looks. "It's not a laborsaving device," she said, "it's a face-saving device."

She had a point. Sweeping is about the lowest-status job on the planet. If the worker uses a broom or rake and works quietly, everyone can ignore him. That's fine for everyone else but maybe not so great for him. The worker is ignorable, invisible, and has zero status. Give him a blower, on the other hand, and he becomes the focus of everyone's attention, the only possible focus. Whether the job gets done any faster is perhaps not what matters most to the worker. His boss has a similar consideration: It's nearly impossible to keep people who have zero-status jobs; give the guy a nice loud machine to boost his ego and maybe he'll stick around for a while.

Saving Labor vs. Saving Face

When we returned from the island, I started to think of other so-called laborsaving devices that may really be face-saving devices in disguise. Consider the ubiquitous word processor, Microsoft Word or whatever you use. Before word processors, managers had to be given secretaries to type their letters, reports, and memos. Today those same managers do their own typing, all made possible by that laborsaving device the word processor. Net saving to the corporation: whatever it used to cost to keep the secretary.

Well, not quite. If it would take a secretary without word processing an hour to type a given report, the manager with word processor can probably also get it done in an hour. More than half of that time is properly considered composition time, work that the manager would have had to do anyway. But what about the rest? What about the time that the manager fiddles with margins, corrects spelling, worries the table into position so it doesn't break across pages? All that is truly clerical work that is now performed by a boss instead of a lower-level person. While we're at it, what about the time that same manager spends installing the program, resolving its weird conflict with the spreadsheet program, looking up the rules for footnotes and other seldom-used features, trying to figure out how to flow text around a graphic?

The word processor is a laborsaving device (please don't

take mine away!), but it has also served a face-saving role, enabling us to transfer a class of what was previously considered clerical work up to higher-paid workers. It's not at all obvious that companies have come out entirely ahead by this switch.

Word processing is just one example. Most of the neat things that your desktop computer does for you today were, in the pre-computer world, handled by clerks, typists, mail room workers, librarians, researchers, and interns, people who typically made a lot less money than you do. Today your PC does some of their work, but you have to drive it, you have to serve *its* needs.

Use of face-saving schemes to push clerical work upward (usually to managers or to knowledge workers) has given us organizations that are critically starved of low-level support. Workers with six-figure incomes are standing in line at copiers, and sorting and filing and generally doing work that could be done by a clerk. I seldom visit a company anymore that could not be made more efficient by the introduction of even a few gofers. When a low-level employee off-loads someone who makes six or eight times as much, the organization is a big winner.

The Problem with Gofers

But let's come to grips with the heart of the problem here: The gofer is *overhead*. You may hire him today, but he's sure to be gone again with the next cost-reduction exercise. We have become so obsessed with getting rid of people who are burdened with the characterization *overhead* that we have ended up with organizations where many high-priced knowledge workers and managers are spending as much as a quarter of their time being their own overhead. Is this an economy?

An absence of low-level support becomes even more important when knowledge workers are arrayed in teams. Consider a project made up of five developers:

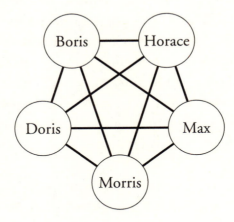

The five have divided up the work among themselves. For such a small group, there is probably no way to divide the work without all team members having at least some interaction with each of the others. So each person has four people to interact with, and the total of all interaction paths is ten.

If we now note that each of the five developers is 20 percent used up doing low-level support, we can envision a slightly trimmer variant of the project by introducing one clerical support person:

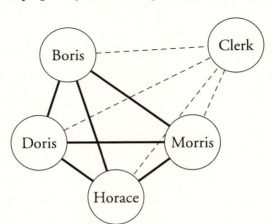

Here we have four developers and only six possible interaction paths among them. In addition, each of the developers has interaction with the clerical person, but this is a much thinner interaction and uses up considerably less of the developers' brainpower.

By dividing up the work into four pieces instead of five, the total time spent serving the interactions is reduced. The capacity of the four-person team plus clerk is thus greater than that of the five-person team. Four developers plus a clerk also cost less than a five-developer team.

Life at the Top

Early in the spring of 1998, I got a call from the new dean of arts and sciences at the University of Maine. She was proposing to convoke an ad hoc group of local "digerati" to advise her on the formation of a new Information Sciences curriculum for the school. I unhesitatingly signed on. During our introductory meeting over lunch, I asked her one of my standard consultant's questions: "Deborah, if I followed you around during a typical workday, what would I see?"

She paused for only a moment before replying, "You'd see a woman who spends at least a third of each day being her own clerk, standing in front of a copier, filing, running errands . . ." She went on to explain that due to economies in the university budget, the dean had no support staff. Whatever needed to be done around the office, she was the only choice to do it.

I find the image of "dean making copies" rather troubling. It's as much a commonplace of the industrial scene as of academia. It may be apparent in your workplace as well. How many of your high-priced managers and engineers and developers and designers are busy being their own clerks as you read these words? How much of your own time is spent that way? I hope you're asking yourself, "What's wrong with this picture?"

12

The Second Law of Bad Management

NOBODY IS GOING to read a chapter on the second law of anything without first knowing what the first law is, so let's get that out of the way immediately.

First Law of Bad Management

If something isn't working, do more of it.

The First Law of Bad Management was observed by consultant and author Jerry Weinberg in the 1990s. On a political level, the First Law explains the conduct of America's war on drugs, among other things. (Maybe it explains *everything* that happens in politics.)

In corporations, First Law abuse is a direct result of trying to manage without benefit of talent. Talented managers are largely immune to this stuff; they're all sense organ, constantly attuned to the effect their leadership is having on their people, constantly adjusting and refining their focus for maximum effect. If something isn't working, they stop doing it and try something else. Managers without such talent find themselves relying on formulas and "principles" of management. They reason, "This thing I'm trying to do *should* work; the fact that it isn't working probably suggests that I'm doing it halfheartedly." And so they do more of whatever they've been doing.

While the First Law is amusing and certainly explains some of the worst organizational fiascoes, it is intrinsically pathological. Thus, it doesn't provide useful guidance to basically capable managers who are striving to become better. My consulting work puts me in constant contact with such good people. I see them succeed and I sometimes see them fail. I try to help them capitalize on their strengths and combat their weaknesses. My purpose in this chapter is to offer a concise observation to help these good managers avoid one of the dumbest and yet most common and damaging errors of management.

A Dumb Thing We All Do

Looking back over the worst failures of my own and my colleagues' management careers, I'm struck by the fact that there is one innocent-seeming sin common to them all. It's something we've all done at one time or another. You've done it yourself.

Second Law of Bad Management

Put yourself in as your own utility infielder.

The inclination to do this is particularly pronounced in today's overstressed un-"slack" organization. You've been trimmed and cut and reduced in staff, your overhead has been slenderized and all operations made superefficient. The result is that the person who used to be responsible for whatever underneath you is now gone. All the rest of your people are busy as hell; you don't want to further burden them with another task, particularly not one that upper management found to be of so little importance that they "trimmed" the person who was doing it. Yet that "whatever" still has to be done. Oh well, you add it to your own burden and do it yourself. On the org chart we now see:

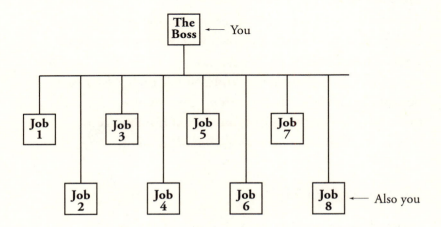

There are two things about this practice that need to be made clear:

1. Why it is the disaster that it is
2. Why we do it anyway

The Joke About Managers

Assigning yourself to an unfilled position in your domain means that you unassign yourself (at least partially) from the task of managing that domain. It shouldn't be necessary to say this to any manager, but unfortunately it is: Management matters. Yes, the uncovered task matters too, but not as much. I have known managers who took on as many as three full jobs reporting to their own management position. Needless to say, the lower-level jobs were badly performed and there was no management at all.

Why do managers need to be told that management matters? At least in the United States and western Europe, there is a strange lore about management that in spite of the substantial salaries paid for it, it really isn't essential to the proper running of the organization. In fact, the lore tells us, management is often *in the way*. I have almost never been in an organization where there weren't little jokes about this: "You can get a ton of work done around here when the Big Boss Lady is out of town," or "Somebody persuade Lawrence to take his vacation next week and we might actually be able to make the deadline." These are not just jokes told about us by our staff people; they are jokes that we tell as well.

The little jokes wouldn't be funny enough to tell if there weren't at least a germ of truth behind them. The germ of truth is this: Managers don't *perform* any of the services or *make* any of the products that our customers pay for. It's the people who report to them that do this work. So each time a manager intervenes in a worker's day, it distracts that worker temporarily from revenue-producing activities. The distraction is probably useful in the long run (because, for example, it effects some new way of doing the work), but in the short run it distracts. In the short term it's just a bother.

The lore may be everywhere, but that doesn't mean you have to buy into it yourself. To do your job correctly and well, you need to foster an attitude that is quite the opposite. You need to understand that management (the management that you provide) is utterly essential. It is. Good management is the lifeblood of the healthy corporate body. Getting rid of it to save cost is like losing weight by giving blood.

Flight from Challenge

We don't do this dumb Second Law thing only because we forget how essential management really is. There are other, much graver causes. The first of these is safety. In a sufficiently overstressed organization, it is positively *unsafe* to manage. Only the work itself—the lowest-level work, such as making product—keeps you safe. So if you manage at all, that has to be a part-time task. The rest of the time you are making product, bringing in revenue. Bringing in revenue makes you safe; the time you spend managing therefore won't count too heavily against you . . . *provided* you keep it to a minimum. This is hardly a formula for thoughtful management.

We also assign ourselves to lower-level work because we're fleeing from challenge. Yes, I know, we all love a good challenge, but that doesn't mean we don't sometimes get cold feet and look for a way out. The challenges of management are daunting: They lead us into the scarily intangible world of people relations, motivation, societal formation, conflict, and conflict resolution.

In my own case, I was promoted into a management position, fresh from a technological job where there were *no* intangibles. I had been a real-time system designer just before my promotion. Systems design is deliciously black-and-white: Your design works or it doesn't. It is sufficiently flexible and accommodating to change or it isn't. You may not know this perfectly at design time, but the implementation phase, which comes next, will quickly prove your design acceptable (even elegant) or not. There are few nuances.

But management is all nuance. Why on earth is Maria so irritable? What's the tension between Armand and Elwood? Is Danny looking for a new job, and what will we do if he leaves? Have I sold the due date as difficult but doable, or is everybody giggling at my naïveté? Did I hit the right tone in my briefing? Is my boss suddenly out of favor, and what does that mean to me?

While I was still coming to grips with all this, one of my designers upped and quit. I unhesitatingly covered the job myself. Whew, what a relief. Now I was not only a manager, but able to spend my days doing sublimely black-and-white work. It seemed like the best of all worlds. But it wasn't. I was walking away from the challenge of management to return to work I knew cold. The relief it gave me was the relief of retreat.

Why Management Is Hard

We all grapple with Second Law temptations at some time in our management careers. To rise above them, we need to face up to an important truth: Management is hard, and not because there is so much work to do (an overworked manager is almost certainly doing work he/she shouldn't be doing). Management is hard because the skills are inherently difficult to master. Your mastery of them will affect your organization more than anything going on under you. Running away from the challenge doesn't help.

13
Culture of Fear

I N *THE NAME OF THE ROSE,* Umberto Eco's captivating mystery
story set in the fourteenth century, monks have been turning
up murdered in a monastery known for its huge archival library. A visiting scholar, William of Baskerville, has heard a ru-
mor that there is a copy in the library (the only surviving copy
on earth) of Aristotle's *Treatise on Comedy.* There is reason to believe that all the monks who have been killed had come in contact with the manuscript. This leads him to suspect the head
librarian, Jorge, of being the murderer.

William's suspicion is borne out and he confronts Jorge,
who tells him that the manuscript is just too dangerous, that all
would be lost if its terrifying contents were ever to escape into
the population at large.

"If this book were to become . . . had become an object for
open interpretation, we would have crossed the last boundary,"
Jorge tells him. For it is Aristotle's heretical position, he con-
tinues, that laughter is an *admirable* and *desirable* thing.

"But what frightened you in this discussion of laughter?" William asks him.

"Laughter, for a few minutes, distracts the villein [common person] from fear. But law is imposed by fear, whose true name is the fear of God. This book could strike the Luciferine spark that would set a new fire to the whole world."

Laughter dispels fear, Jorge goes on, and fear is our only real hope of salvation. "What would we be, we sinful creatures, without fear, perhaps the most foresighted and most loving of the divine gifts?"

In the end, the *Treatise* is lost in a fire that Jorge sets to consume the entire library (so we're all safe, I guess).

The Divine Gift

The *Treatise* is gone, but something else did survive the fire: Jorge's warped notion that fear is a divine gift. How else to explain the prominent and respected position that fear is given in so many organizations? How else to explain the "culture of fear" that dominates the workplace for so many?

Among the characteristics of the Culture of Fear organization are these:

1. It is not safe to say certain things (e.g., "I have serious doubts that this quota can be met"). And truth is no excuse for saying them.

2. In fact, being right in your doubts proves that you must be the reason that the fondest wishes of those above you did not come true.

3. Goals are set so aggressively that there is virtually no chance of achieving them.

4. Power is allowed to trump common sense.

5. Anyone can be abused and abased for a failure to knuckle under.

6. The people who are fired are, on average, more competent than the people who aren't.

7. The surviving managers are a particularly angry lot. Everyone is terrified of crossing them.

I hope that as you read these points you're inclined to think they present a truly extreme picture. I hope this, since it suggests that yours is not a Culture of Fear organization. (If the portrait I've drawn does not seem extreme to you, you have my sympathies.)

The Angry Manager

If you work for a healthy enough company, you may be having trouble believing that a Culture of Fear occurs frequently enough in organizations to make it worth writing about. I don't have handy data that show, for example, that 14.3 percent or 8.8 percent or 26.923 percent of corporate cultures are so perverse. But I offer the following as an informal indicator that angry management—just to take the last point of my numbered list—is a fairly common phenomenon. My indicator comes from that bellwether of all meaningful American trends, the glossy ad section of an airline magazine: An ad that appeared regularly in the airline mags for years showed a male upper manager, a "suit," seated at a table surrounded by other upper management types. The guy is absolutely livid: his skin is flushed, veins popping, mouth twisted into a jagged line. He is glaring out toward a subordinate and asking in wrathful exasperation, "What's your excuse this time?" The other managers at the table look down in embarrassment.

Lower down on the page we see that this is an ad for a day-timer, a scheduling aid. It's one of those fancy ones with lots of features. The intended message of the ad, I guess, is that when you're late on something and the boss gets mad at you, it probably isn't your fault at all; it's probably the fault of your inadequate day book. The stupid thing probably has insufficient dividers, tabs and clear pockets, or maybe it's bound with not enough rings. If only you'd get yourself a really modern-day book like the one shown in the ad, the text tells you, such scenes would never have to happen to you again. So get off your duff and buy a new day book.

Well, that's the point the ad is *trying* to make. The point it conveyed to me is a little different. I think the ad is all about managerial anger. Notice that nowhere in the copy is there any acknowledgment of the brutality of the situation portrayed. This is a really ugly scene. The boss is calling down an employee, in public. This manager is furious and venting it in front of everyone. Some poor bastard (you, the ad implies) is withering under the onslaught. Yet the copy writers didn't seem to feel any need to distance themselves from what was happening, no need to assure you that, "We really don't condone this kind of extreme managerial abuse, but . . ."

Suppose that the picture had showed instead an angry father about to rip into his kid with the buckle end of a belt. Suppose further that it was just an ad from a belt company. You can bet that the belt company's copy writers would have rushed to assure you that they didn't approve of this kind of child abuse. They would have had to distance themselves from blatantly unacceptable and antisocial behavior. But the scene of the angry manager is offered up as all part of a normal day's work. No need to remark upon it, this is simply one more unfortunate instance of something that happens all the time in the workplace. It's just the way things are.

The fact that we don't require any explanation for this kind of managerial tantrum means that we take it for granted. Oh, it certainly isn't desirable, we sigh, but it does happen. Yes, it does; it's part of a Culture of Fear.

Angry managers are losers, hapless incompetents who are in way over their heads and haven't got the faintest idea how to lead. In the long run, they will come tumbling down under the weight of their own fury. In the short run, however, they tend to cluster. That means that a few organizations end up with way more than their share. I mention this because from the inside of this kind of culture, it may not be at all obvious that the level of abuse you see around you isn't common everywhere. It isn't. If you've stumbled into such a situation, get out. Life is too short.

Once established, the Culture of Fear gets in the way of everything that is healthy or worthwhile. Growth is stunted, change (improvement) becomes nearly impossible, morale is in the Dumpster. Meaningful achievement is always just out of reach. Good people leave and new good people stay away in droves.

Of all the many bad effects that the Culture of Fear engenders, I shall provide detail here on only one. I want to focus you on this one problem because it is at once so damaging and yet so poorly understood. It is what I call . . .

The Paradox of Overstaffing

Remember that the subject here—the subject of all of Part II—is the effect of stress on organizations. One of the most obvious causes of stress is understaffing. Payrolls are cut, overhead positions combined, and the result is that you're forever trying to do with nine people what used to be done with eleven. That certainly is a common enough kind of stress.

It's tempting to say that overstressed organizations are *always* understaffed; that that's where all the stress comes from in the first place. It's tempting, but it isn't entirely so. There are also situations where *over*staffing is the problem, where overstaffing is both the cause of the stress and part of our response to it.

To understand this, imagine yourself recently appointed as manager of a brand-new project. The project's goal is to bring out an entirely new and drastically different version of the company's backbone product. Of course, there is no way that such a project can be conducted at anything less than a ferocious gallop. No sir. There is a lot at stake here and this project needs to be done yesterday. Well, it can't be done yesterday, but it *must* be done by end of third quarter of next year. You can take upper management's word for that. In fact, the president himself has gone on record that the product will ship by next September 30. He dropped that at a press conference, and now all the business press has reported it.

To your experienced eye, September 30 looks downright impossible. It's not only an unrealistic schedule, it isn't even a credible goal. You don't believe in it and neither does anyone else. So, ever hopeful, you go to your boss for a bit of leeway. You tell her that the September 30 date just isn't in the cards. "It's got to be," she tells you firmly. "We'll just give you all the people you need to make the date. How many do you need?"

"Well," you say, "I was thinking of three designers, at least one with interface design expertise, plus one systems guy (an architecture specialist), a test and Q.A. person, and myself. That's six at the beginning. Then staffing up from May or June to about twenty. But even with that ideal staff . . ."

"Take sixty," your boss says. "Sixty today and up to a hundred fifty by year-end. That ought to do it."

And there's the dilemma. The gauntlet is down. Are you a

big-league manager who can run a staff of 60 to 150 people, or are you just another little leaguer who can only manage a teensy-weensy staff? One thing is sure: If you stick to your guns and run the project with an initial half dozen in staff, then missing the date will be blamed entirely on your unwillingness to step up to the challenge.

The nature of project work is that whatever it is you're about to build, the early conceptual phases are crucial. But this kind of conceptual work can't be done with a crowd of people. A staff of no more than six might make perfect sense while the first-cut design decisions are made. Burdening the project with an extra fifty people at this stage will only make the work go slower. Or worse: With that many people on your budget, your every incentive as manager is to find something (anything!) for them to do. All your available choices here are bad. Anything you assign that many people to do locks you into conceptual decisions that haven't yet been thought out. You're forced to partition the whole—this kind of partitioning is the essence of design—along lines that are dictated by personnel-loading considerations rather than design considerations. The result is sure to be a mediocre or poor design, something that will encumber the project from this point on.

Look what's happened here. You've ended up staffing the project with so many people that it's bound to take longer to finish than it would have with a smaller staff. But that doesn't matter. Meeting the deadline is not what this is all about. What this is about is *looking like you're trying your damnedest to meet the deadline.* In this age of "lean and mean," it is positively unsafe for you to run the project with a lean (optimal) staff.

That's the kind of craziness that comes from corporate stress and the Culture of Fear. And it gets worse. Read on . . .

14

Litigation

IT'S NO SECRET that companies, particularly U.S. companies, are more litigious today than ever before. What may not be so obvious is that the Culture of Fear plays an important role in much of modern litigation. In my work as an expert witness and litigation consultant, for example, I seldom see a case where there isn't at least one Culture of Fear organization involved. And since we expert witnesses are a close-knit fraternity, I get to hear juicy details on many more cases than I can work on firsthand. My sense is that perhaps a tenth of all U.S. corporations are substantially fearful, but more than half of those involved in litigation are true Culture of Fear organizations.

The Litigation Game

Just in case you've been lucky enough to avoid litigation so far in your career, let me sketch in a few common details. Corporate litigations are enormously expensive, typically costing the two parties a total in legal fees that dwarfs whatever settlement is finally imposed. Neither side wins, everybody loses. That is almost a defining characteristic of modern litigation: Everybody always loses. Nobody ever comes out ahead as a result of litigation. Legal fees are only part of the cost; the litigants may end up using as much or more manpower on the litigation as was expended on the entire contract under dispute. Litigations drag on forever, often longer than the term of the original contract. When the whole sad charade is over, morale of both organizations is depressed. All involved know they have just wasted years of their lives on something pointless and destructive.

So why do they do it? Why enter into a litigation? When things go awry, why not just take your lumps and get on with the business of business? In my experience, there are two important reasons why litigation happens in spite of the most dismal prospects for it ever achieving anything worthwhile:

1. Litigation can be an effective way to deflect blame. A failure that cannot be blamed on someone outside the organization must be accepted within the organization. And some highly political organizations exact a very high price for that.

2. Litigation can be a consequence of an intrinsically flawed contract. The underlying agreement at the heart of the dispute leaves one party egregiously victimized by the other from the git-go. The redress that the aggrieved party seeks is more a matter of principle than profit.

As you can see, these two causes don't appear to have a lot in common. And, to add to the confusion, litigations of the first type are often obliged to masquerade as litigations of the second type. No matter which is the real cause, a Culture of Fear is sure to be involved.

Litigation as a Means of Passing Blame

Let's say Buyer Corporation contracts with Seller Corporation for construction of a Somethingorother. Making Something-orothers is the particular forte of Seller Corp., not Buyer Corp. That's why the contract happened in the first place. But Buyer Corp. still has a role to play in successful completion of the contract: Buyer will almost certainly have to specify requirements for the Somethingorother to make sure it will receive exactly what it wants; it may have responsibility for acceptance-testing the delivered result consistent with the requirement. Buyer is also responsible for its selection of Seller. Finally, Buyer always has the responsibility to be sure that it really had a use for the Somethingorother, that it won't turn out to be just another expensive fiasco.

Suppose that Buyer Corp. fails in any one of its responsibilities. Failure doesn't just happen, it's somebody's fault. Somebody was responsible for specifying the correct requirement, for example. If the requirement was imprecise, vague as to essential details, or just wrong, then that responsible party at Buyer is left holding the bag.

In a healthy organization, a certain amount of failure is okay. At Microsoft, for example, there has long been an almost official policy of "sink, then swim." People are loaded down with so much responsibility that they sink (fail). Then they have a chance to rest up, to analyze and modify their own performance. Finally, they are loaded again with a comparable amount of responsibility, but this time they succeed. If they don't sink the first time, that just shows they weren't challenged enough. They can be sure that the next time out they will be challenged a lot more aggressively. To the extent that this policy is applied company-wide, Microsoft seems to be run as an Outward Bound adventure. Finding your weaknesses by failing is not just incidental; it is designed into the corporate philosophy.

Healthy companies know that they have to allow people to fail without assessing blame. They have to do that or else no one will take on anything that's not a sure bet. Healthy companies know that, but Culture of Fear companies do not. In a Culture of Fear company, failure *must* be rewarded with punishment. ("What would we be, we sinful creatures, without fear?") A typical punishment is that you get fired. If the people above you are insufficiently powerful, some of them may get fired as well. This creates a powerful incentive to pass responsibility for failure on by blaming someone outside the organization. When Seller, in my example, delivers exactly what Buyer Corp. asked for in its erroneous specification, the incentive is to sue Seller for delivering such a useless Somethingorother.

You might think that such a suit would be doomed to fail, that Seller Corp. will trot out the erroneous specification, prove that the whole melancholy business was Buyer's fault, and thus win the litigation. If you think that, you haven't been paying attention. Nobody ever wins a litigation. Everybody always loses. To make matters worse, litigation is such a crapshoot that the relatively innocent party may end up losing worse than the relatively guilty party. This happens because today's contracts are so technical and complex that our courts are overwhelmed by the issues. The results are more likely to be decided by quality of the legal team, or the relative comprehensibility of one side's contention, than by the true merits of the case.

When it's all done, Buyer has suffered the failed project

and then suffered further losses due to the litigation. But some people within Buyer Corp. may have successfully deflected blame from themselves to Seller. Even if the court disagrees, by the end of the infinitely long legal process, the guilty parties at Buyer have almost certainly been promoted out of the domain of responsibility or have left the company on their own schedule.

Context for Blame

The chemistry of Culture of Fear organizations seems to call for a fixed minimum amount of blame. In some companies, this minimum may even be written into policy. Consider, for example, G.E.'s policy that all managers be evaluated every year and the bottom 10 percent be fired. Prospering in such an environment can take two forms: Either you have to do relatively well, or some of your peers have to do relatively badly. Any failure by managers beside you on the org chart thus has the effect of reducing pressure on you. In such an environment, there is a natural inclination to view with suspicion anything that would constitute a big win for any other manager.

In most of the litigations I see, there is serious conflict between rival stakeholders inside one (sometimes inside both) of the litigating organizations. There might be a sales department at Buyer Corp., for example, that stands to gain substantially if a successful Somethingorother were to be installed. There might also be a marketing department that stands to lose. And so the marketing department (particularly if Buyer is a Culture of Fear company) imposes a few restrictions of its own on the requirement, or contests some of the sales department's most valued features. The requirement is bulked up, watered down, or made vague to satisfy both conflicted parties, and the result is lateness or overrun or delivery of something useless to everyone. Whoops, time to deflect upper management's attention by suing Seller Corp.

So far, my example has shown only the buyer, not the seller, to be the relatively blameworthy party. Clearly, it can be the other way around. Seller may fail due to its own incompetence to deliver a relatively well specified Somethingorother, and try to get off the hook by suing Buyer for a handful of late-arriving changes. Buyer will then argue valiantly in court that the amount of change was normal and only to be expected. It may be right in this, but it hardly matters. Everybody loses except those whose main goal was to deflect blame.

Flawed Contract

Many of the contracts that eventually end up in litigation are so hopelessly flawed that neither party should ever have signed them. The most common flaw of these contracts is an unrealistic price and/or schedule. Buyer and Seller may bind themselves, for example, in a contract calling for delivery of a custom Somethingorother in less time than any Somethingorother has ever been completed before. You may understand why Buyer would enter into such a contract, but what about Seller?

In order to understand Seller's motives, we need to look well below the corporate level to the subordinate organization that will perform the work. Under the gun to show profit and growth (perhaps in a weakening market), this organization is encouraged to best its competition by offering lower price or earlier delivery. Someone within the organization is responsible for getting the work done, for actually building the Somethingorother on time and on budget. He/she tries to say the unpalatable truth that the time and money allocated for the work are plain insufficient. In a Culture of Fear organization, such doubts are stifled or shouted down. "Don't tell me it can't be done, goddammit. It *will* be done. If you can't do it, I'll get somebody competent in here who can."

The person doing the shouting is someone in authority, someone higher up on the org chart. Authority here has more force than reality . . . for a while. Eventually, reality weighs in, and the result is another fine mess. Time for litigation.

Buyer probably initiates litigation in this case, since it has been woefully wronged. It was promised delivery in eleven months and now, thirty-five months and a lot of add-on dollars later, there is still nothing done. Although it hasn't got a leg to stand on, Seller will probably countersue. In some cases, third parties get sued as well, particularly if either of the litigants is effectively judgment-proof and one of the subcontract suppliers has got deep pockets. The merits of the case will be lost in the confusion of the technology, the awkward wording of a few e-mails, and the ingenious legal tacks taken on all sides. If there isn't enough there to confuse a judge, one party or the other is sure to insist that the case be heard by a jury.

Both Sides (Deserve to) Lose

In this example, Seller Corp. is the rascal. They were the ones who shouted down the voice of reason and bound themselves to do what was impossible from the start. They did that for the most venal motive: to stop Buyer from contracting with a competitor at what, in retrospect, might have been a fair price and schedule. They made a terrible deal in order to have the short-term benefit of winning the contract. Then they tried to negotiate for more time, hold up Buyer for more money, and deflect blame any way they could.

Seller is largely culpable here, but the other party to the contract may have incurred some responsibility as well. I am not trying to predict how the court will decide, only to point out that Buyer may have brought some of the disaster on itself by negotiating too strenuously. But hold on there, you might argue, isn't that what negotiating is all about? Those negotiating seminars you see advertised so much would certainly support such a view; they teach that the negotiation is not really successful until you have positively screwed the other side. Screwing the other side, of course, is a perfectly reasonable goal in a Culture of Fear organization. And that's why so many of them end up in litigation. But in the wider world it doesn't make sense at all.

If you are determined to avoid litigation, then you need to negotiate with an entirely different strategy. The strategy I would urge upon you is what the author Verna Allee calls the *principle of fair exchange.*[1] Simply stated, this principle requires you to arrive at an agreement that would be equally acceptable to you from either side. In other words, you would be willing to sign as either party. Buyer Corp., in the example above, has responsibility to know whether the price and schedule offered by Seller are doable. If they aren't, if the terms are weighted too strongly in Seller's favor, Buyer should not enter into the agreement. If Buyer can't understand the whole subject well enough to make that determination, it has no business entering into the contract.

Litigation and Slack

A troubling aspect of many litigations is that employees of the guilty party (or parties) almost always knew that something was amiss. They knew, for example, that the contract was flawed from the beginning, that deadlines or performance targets

---

[1]Allee, Verna, "The Ethics of Knowledge," *Executive Excellence,* May 2000.

were unrealistic, or that they would have to use some artifice along the way to beef up the price. They make devastating witnesses against their own cause because, testifying under oath, they can't conceal their early knowledge. Many of them will have written imprudent (i.e., honest) memos or e-mails to their management, making what eventually will become their litigation opponent's case.

Why do good people get themselves into this dreadful stew? The root cause of bad contracts (contracts in which the principle of fair exchange is not respected) is stress. Someone in authority has trumpeted, "Don't tell me it can't be done by April. I am the vice president!" And so authority is used to trump reality . . . briefly. Those lower down on the totem pole suppress their reservations and try to put on a good face, for a while at least.

A good contract requires slack. If a vendor commits to X by a given date, you act to your own peril to accept that commitment unless you can see that the vendor has left itself sufficient slack. If there are two competing vendors with different prices and the difference is explained by the fact that the cheaper one has cut all slack, then you court the disaster of litigation by choosing the low bidder. Similarly, if you are bidder, you need to know there is sufficient slack in the contract terms to cover reasonably expected risks.

15

Process Obsession

STANDARDS are a very good thing. Consider: Your new Lucent telephone uses the exact same modular connector (RJ-11 in the United States) to plug into the line jack as your older Panasonic phone used. It has the same ten number keys and two special-character keys as your old phone, and they are arrayed in the same 3 × 4 layout. It sends the same multifrequency tones, works on the same signal and ringing voltages, respects the same tip-and-ring wiring convention. If it draws house current, it does so through a standard plug that will fit into your standard wall receptacle. If it didn't respect all these standard conventions, the new phone would be useless; your only option for installing it at all would be to connect to an entire telephone infrastructure supplied by the same maker. Changing anything would force you to change everything.

Widespread and widely respected standards assure that you can drop a Fuji film canister into a Kodak camera and the ensemble will work every bit as well as if you dropped it in a Kodak canister. You can buy floppy disks and tape cassettes and pencil lead and batteries and staples and gasoline and copy paper from any of a host of different providers and never worry about fit. Standards are not just good; they are *essential* to our modern way of life.

Which brings us to the subject of process standards. If standards in everything else are good, why not a standard way to develop an ad campaign, or a standard way to review employee performance, or a standard way to write computer programs, or a standard way to do any of the myriad tasks that make up the modern world of knowledge work? What could be more sensible than adopting one way of doing any particular task and then imposing that way on all employees? The advantage is obvious: We'll be able to switch people from one part of the organization to another and the work procedures will be so familiar that adaptation is easy. (We might even switch them around several times a day!)

There is enough perceived value in this proposition, and enough precedent for it all around us, that our every inclination may be to accept the validity of standard process and set out to standardize everything we do. This can lead to a positive obsession with process. Process obsession is the problem. Process obsession is not just an anomaly that occurs now and again. It is an epidemic. Process obsession is as common in knowledge-worker organizations today as the common cold . . . and, in my opinion, about as desirable.

How-to Standards

It's worth pointing out that the metaphor I used to open this chapter, and the one most generally used to advocate standard process, is a bit stretched when applied to knowledge work. The standards we depend on to give us choice in our lives are all *product* standards. Almost without exception, they are used to constrain the interface characteristic of a product, not the way that product is built. So Fuji is obliged to respect the ISO standard for size and shape of its film containers, for film width and light sensitivity, sprocket hole positions, edge smoothness, and a thousand other characteristics of the product. If they don't, they can't sell that film as 35mm, ASA400, or whatever. The standards do not tell Fuji how to make the film, only how the product has to present itself after it's made. The particular recipe for the film—the series of steps it passes through on the production line—is left entirely to the maker. If Fuji decides to spray-paint the markings onto the canister before the film is inserted, while Kodak prints its markings onto its canister after insertion, that's their business. The standard doesn't touch on the how-tos of film making; only on the character of the end product.

In manufacturing, there are certainly local how-to standards. So a company that extrudes aluminum moldings, for example, would certainly want to adopt a standard way to run all its extrusion stations, regardless of which of the many different molding patterns is being extruded at each one. This standardization of manufacturing process was the particular interest of an early-twentieth-century mechanical engineer named Frederick Winslow Taylor. His 1911 book, *The Principles of Scientific Management,* set out to do for the human aspect of factory work what the principle of interchangeable parts had done for rifles half a century earlier. Taylorism called for rigorous standardization of manual factory activity so that the human pieces of the process would be as interchangeable as the parts of the products.

Beyond Taylorism

With nearly a century under its belt, Taylorism is still alive and well in the manufacturing sector today. I shall argue below that it is particularly ill suited to knowledge work, but there is no question that it is in common use in today's factories. Before passing on to the knowledge sector, however, I beg your indulgence for a moment to look at two manufacturing organizations that have moved beyond Taylorism in the factory.

1. The first of these is Volvo, which during the 1980s hit upon a team-based vehicle assembly scheme that would have given Taylor fits. A team of workers is assigned to a given vehicle from the beginning (at this "beginning," there really is no vehicle, only an empty spot on the assembly line where the vehicle will begin to take shape). The team follows the vehicle all the way along the assembly line. Members of the team change their functions as the vehicle moves along. They weld when welding is called for, bolt on parts, wire in electronic subassemblies, dip and paint and clean, apply upholstery and cushioning and fabric, snap in the windshield, mount the wheels and tires, balance and test, wax and polish. At the end, the team members scratch their signatures with a diamond-tipped pen under one of the fenders.

This is a model that deviates from Taylorism in nearly every way. The vehicle team is made up of generalists, not specialists. Each of them needs to master an extended set of skills. Their days and hours are strikingly varied. Their identification is with one entire vehicle, not with one tiny aspect of all vehicles.

2. My second example is the Post cereal factory in Jonesboro, Arkansas. Here, too, a factory that could be run in strict Taylor methodology is run in an entirely different way. Three shifts are organized into three teams, each responsible for running the factory its own way during its eight hours. Though each team makes the same products and strives toward the same targets as the others, the decisions about how and when the various component activities are carried out are left to the individual teams. The teams even have the authority to close down their lines for brief periods, get together and brainstorm, and invent new ways to get the job done.

In both of these examples, ownership of the process is pushed downward. Instead of being a corporate asset, it is a team asset. Somewhat lost is the flexibility to move people from one team to another, since over time the teams may begin to deviate substantially from each other. Offsetting this loss is a much more interesting workday for the workers, enhanced identification with the product (and its customer), lower turnover, and strongly felt loyalties to the team and to the corporation.

Does this imply that Taylorism is bad for factory work? No, only that it is not the end-all. There is human capital in factory workers too, an ever-increasing amount; preservation of this factory human capital may well require us to rethink the benefits of Taylorism even in the domain for which it was intended.

Star Workers

Knowledge work is a domain for which Taylorism was never intended. Knowledge work is just not very like factory work. There is no assembly line and there never will be, there aren't many fixed rules, values are more subjective, measurements more dubious, judgment is all-important. This is a card game where all the cards are wild. Knowledge work is less like the jobs that Taylor was studying, and more like the job that he himself was doing when he studied them. It involves invention, abstraction, articulation, and skillful management of many human relationships.

In a study of workers at Bell Telephone Laboratories, interviewers asked engineers in one division to identify stars among their peers. They came up with a short list of such stars and set out to determine how their work procedures differed from those of their nonstar counterparts. Surprisingly, the stars approached their work in ways that were not very different from the way their peers did. As a purely mechanical matter, they did the same work pretty much the same way as everyone else. But there were marked differences in how they managed their networks of connections, liaisons to fellow workers whose cooperation was required to get anything done. For example, people tended to return the stars' telephone calls much more quickly. So a star, on average, would receive answers in twenty minutes, while the norm for the whole laboratory was more like four hours. Why did they get better attention from coworkers and colleagues? There was no obvious answer, but they did. Clearly, the stars had long before taken whatever steps were necessary to establish good connections. They had spread around favors, been responsive themselves, nursed relationships, seen to other people's essential human needs.

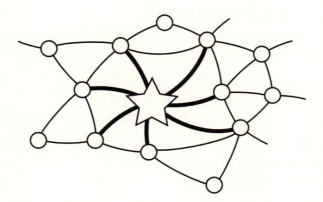

The "stars" had richer connections than their peers . . .

To establish a standardized way of doing any knowledge task, you end up focusing on the mechanics of the task. But the mechanics are a small and typically not very important portion of the whole. How the work goes on inside the nodes of the worker diagram is not nearly so important as how wide and rich are the connections.

Enter Automation

All this is further complicated by the presence of ever-increasing automation in the knowledge-work environment. Each time you add automation, you choose some particularly mechanical component of the work (that's what makes it a good candidate for automation). When the new automation is in place, there is less total work to be done by the human worker, but *what work is left is harder.* That is the paradox of automation: It makes the work harder, not easier. After all, it was the easy stuff that got absorbed into the machine, so what's left is, almost by definition, fuzzier, less mechanical, and more complex. Whatever standard is now introduced to govern the work will dictate (often in elaborate detail) how the few remaining mechanical aspects are to be performed.

Process standards can be a highly emotional matter. There are "process wars," as people begin to feel territorial about their vanishing prerogatives. After a new standard process has been installed, there may be blood in the corridors, a residue of bad feeling all around. After all that hullabaloo, I'm usually underwhelmed by the process itself. In my experience, standard processes for knowledge work are almost always empty at their center. So a new process may tell you, for example, the twenty-nine steps you *must* go through in the interviewing and hiring of a new engineer, but never give you a bit of guidance on the only thing that really matters: Will this guy cut the mustard? I see design standards that don't tell you how to come up with a good design (only how to write it down), employee evaluation standards that don't help you build meaningful long-term relationships with staff, testing standards that don't tell you how to invent a test that is worth running. Each of these standards says, in effect, "I will dictate to you exactly how you must do every aspect of the work . . . except the hard part."

Ownership and Empowerment

Why do companies get hung up on something so ill adapted that it is doomed to fail or, even worse, to be irrelevant? The reason has more to do with our frustrations and fears as managers than with any consideration of efficiency and good practice. Setting a standard for the process establishes ownership. If I am your boss and I impose no standard on you, I've effectively let you own the process. But wait a minute. Who's boss here? I am. So don't I need to own the process? I certainly need to be in control, don't I?

If the term "empowerment" is to have any meaning at all, it means putting process ownership largely into the hands of the people doing the work. That doesn't mean there should be no standard, only that whatever standard evolves should happen at the level of the work itself. Ownership of the standard should be in the hands of those who do the work. That is an ideal, one that you will probably never be able to attain completely, particularly in big companies. But it is always worth striving toward.

It's also scary. In my management seminars, I often query groups of managers about empowerment. (They're all in favor.) Then I ask these young managers, "When you empower a subordinate, do you yourself lose any control?" They gravely answer that no, they do not lose control. But that answer makes no sense at all. Empowerment always implies transfer of control to the person empowered and out of the hands of the manager. That doesn't mean you give up all control, only some. You can't empower anyone without taking chances. The power you've granted is the power to err. If that person messes up, you take the consequences. Looked at from the opposite perspective, it is this capacity to injure the person above you that makes empowerment work. It leaves the empowered person thinking, "Oh my God, if I fail at this, my boss is going to look like a chump for trusting me." There is little else in the work experience with so much capacity to motivate.

Process standardization from on high is disempowerment. It is a direct result of fearful management, allergic to failure. It tries to avoid all chance of failure by having key decisions made by a guru class (those who set the standards) and carried out mechanically by the regular folk. As defense against failure, standard process is a kind of armor. The more worried you are about failure, the heavier the armor you put on. But armor always has a side effect of reduced mobility. The overarmored organization has lost the ability to move and move quickly. When this happens, standard process is the cause of lost mobility. It is, however, not the root cause. The root cause is fear.

16
Quality

OKAY, so standard process, Culture of Fear, under- and over-staffing, pressure, and overtime are all part of the Dark Side. But quality? The corporate Quality Program? The "quality is job one" mentality? How can these be anything but wonderful?

Quality has not just been the mind-set for the past decade; it has risen to the status of movement. The Quality Movement today is pushing a billion dollars a year of conferences, books, programs, seminars, urgent exhortations, and cloying posters.

Most of this is little more than lip service. Paying lip service to quality doesn't necessarily make it better. Quality in this sense is a lot like apple pie and motherhood. The United States and other Western cultures have spent the last fifty years extolling the virtues and talking up the importance of apple pie and motherhood, and yet during this same period both apple pie and motherhood have suffered a precipitous decline in their fortunes. The store-bought, packaged, plastic apple pie we eat today would make our grandmothers cringe. And motherhood, particularly in the ghettos and poor suburban neighborhoods, has become, for many, more of a curse than a blessing. This in spite of our constantly stated affirmation. We might as well have saved our breath.

My problem with the Quality Movement is not that it costs too much or that it saps too much energy out of our organizations. My problem is that it is too little service and too much lip service. And, as I will show in this chapter, our ubiquitous quality improvement programs just make real quality improvement harder.

An absence of slack makes quality programs seem like a cruel joke. When there is neither time nor staff to cope with work that runs more slowly than expected, then the cost of lateness is paid out of quality. There is no other degree of freedom. Lost time in the early or middle stages is offset by reductions in the later work, and quality suffers. My beef with organizations that make this tradeoff is not only that they put out shoddy products; my main objection is that they never stop proclaiming their dedication to quality while they're making the very tradeoffs that make quality impossible.

The Best Product Ever Made Is . . .

First of all, let's all admit that quality is a good thing. You know this if your Toyota has given you 160,000 miles of trouble-free transportation, or if you've got three generations of Macs in a closet that you can't throw away because the amazing things still run fine. You know this if you've ever used a product that was so beautifully made that it gave you a chill of pleasure just to hold it in your hand.

A good definition of quality might be handy here, but—definitions being (by definition) rather abstract—I propose instead to give you an example. The example I've chosen comes from my experience as a user of computer software products. We know that the software industry turns out some fine products and some lemons. We might assume that among all the good software products, one is the best. But which one is it? No one to my knowledge has ever even come up with a nomination. That's a shame, because the best piece of software ever written could be a fine model for anyone who sets out to build something better still. Before I give my own nomination for best, I need to mention that (1) I do not hold stock in the company that made this product, or any company that profits from the sale of it, and (2) I have never consulted for the maker or any of its allied organizations. In what follows, you may quibble with my choice of best, but I hope you will find value in my rationale.

The best software product ever made is . . . Adobe Photoshop. In case you don't know it, Photoshop is a facility for operating upon digital images. It allows you to change exposure, brightness and contrast, color balances and saturations. You can shift hue, refocus, crop, sharpen, blur, highlight, remove red-eye, adjust gray levels, color-separate, print and package any digital image or portion thereof. You can merge images, superimpose, add shadows, overprint, collage, solarize, negativize, filter, and generally alter images with such precision and exactness that the whole concept of a photo as legal evidence is forever after thrown into question.

Just imagine that you and someone very dear to you have just spent a lovely day on a deserted beach. To preserve the moment, you've taken a number of photos of each other, shooting carefully for easy, relaxed expressions and placement to make best use of the surroundings. Let's say the photos come out as well as you could ever have hoped: You've each caught one great photo of the other. Of course, since you were alone, there is no shot of the two of you together. What a shame.

But wait, maybe Photoshop can come to the rescue. All you have to do is digitize the two photos and then extract one person's image to merge into the other photo:

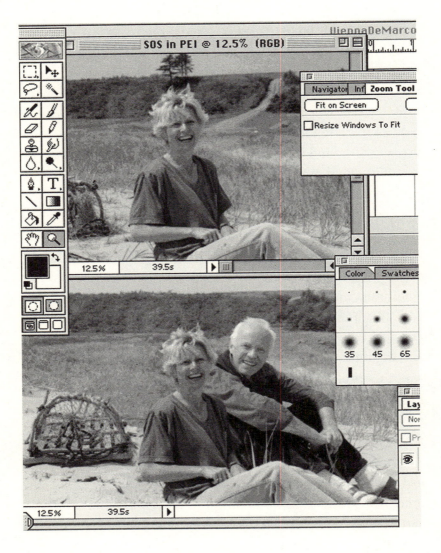

In the image shown above, I have inserted myself behind my then fiancée, to produce a composite of the pair of us on the beach on Prince Edward Island. Since we were married in

Charlottetown later that day, the picture has come to be our wedding photo. We treasure it every bit as much as if it had been shot directly with the two of us sitting together.

Look what's happened here: A new product has not just assisted work that used to be done some other way; it has transformed the whole way people think about the possibilities.

My reason for going out so far on a limb as to specifically name an all-time best software product (believe me, those of my clients who are in the software business will not be amused) is to have one concrete example to illustrate the process used in judging anything to be of high quality. I have chosen Photoshop as best for the following reasons:

1. It is unique; when it first appeared, it was *utterly* unique.

2. It redefines the whole notion of photo processing.

3. It even redefines the way you think about photos. (Don't throw away that snap that is great of Helen but awful of Murray. Just merge it with another that has a better Murray.)

4. It allows you to do things that were barely imaginable before.

5. It is deeply thought out; in particular, its use of channels is almost infinitely extensible and usable in ever-increasing numbers of ways.

6. It is fully implemented; for example, its "undo" feature can undo even the most complex action.

7. Its human interface sticks in the mind—you almost never need to use the manual.

8. It is revolutionary in the way it affords an interface for third-party add-on providers.

9. It is solid as a rock.

I've given you the first nine reasons for my choice, more or less in order of importance. Note that of the nine, only the very last one has anything to do with absence of defect. That's my point. Product quality has almost nothing to do with defects or their lack. Oh sure, a basically good product may be marred by defects (think of your Internet browser, whichever one you use). But real quality is far more a matter of what it does for you and how it changes you than whether it is perfectly free of flaws. So that browser, even though it crashes maddeningly often, should be considered a quality product. That's why you use it so much. Its quality is most of all a function of its usefulness.

The Corporate Quality Program

Real quality has little to do with defects, but our so-called quality programs have everything to do with defects. The corporate Quality Program, at its heart, is a mechanism for driving out defects. When it succeeds, it will help you produce products that are defect-free, or nearly so. But are those products good for anything? Maybe yes and maybe no, but either way, it's not due to the Quality Program.

That's my gripe with Quality Programs. They focus on one easy and actionable aspect of quality and ignore everything else. They concentrate on something that is almost incidental to real quality and ignore what really matters. If my nine-point list of Photoshop's quality were generalizable, it would suggest that a real Quality Program should spend one-ninth or less of its resources on defect prevention and removal, and the rest on assuring product uniqueness, usefulness, market impact, change of customer work modes, etc.

Well, what of it? Something is better than nothing, you might think, and so a Quality Program that deals with only a ninth of what real quality means is still that much better than no program at all. Ah, but that assumes that such a program has no worsening effect on the other quality factors. Can you really assume that about your Quality Program? Consider the following awful possibilities:

- ❑ Defect prevention and removal efforts may add sufficient overhead to the overall process so that it is too slow and unresponsive to market needs.
- ❑ A proposed new technology may be judged initially more error-prone than the current approach, and so the quality targets mitigate against its adoption, even though the new technology could make possible a whole new family of highly useful products.
- ❑ Any risky new endeavor is likely to result in an increasing pattern of defects; the Quality Program thus may pit itself squarely against risk-taking efforts.
- ❑ The Quality Program may engender a Quality Assurance organization which has the secondary effect of reducing quality control efforts within its partner organizations.

More important than these relative quibbles is the co-opting effect that Quality Programs typically have: Since they lay claim to whatever magic the word "quality" has, they make it impossible to advance a quality argument for anything except defect-freeness. The loser here is the organization as a whole. The strongest argument for new product integrity and usefulness has been effectively silenced.

Quality and Calendar Time

Suppose you were to read in the newspaper that your country's brand-new air traffic control system was to be developed on a "highly aggressive" schedule. What's your response to that? Is there any little voice inside you whispering, "Wait a minute here; let's not hurry those folks along too much"? (If you don't hear such a voice, I guess you don't fly much.)

Quality takes time. Even quality in the "defects only" sense takes time. So you might assume that a Quality Program for a development effort would, as its most important task, assure the quality of the schedule. I always assumed that. But so far, I have never come across a corporate Quality Program or a Quality Assurance organization that made any pretense of judging reasonableness of the time allocated for the work. What typically happens is that the schedule is set *before* the quality people come on board. Anything they do in the interests of quality happens after the date (which makes quality either possible or impossible) has been set.

Seems all backward to me. I'd much prefer the opposite, in which the Quality Assurance organization did its work *only* at the beginning of the project, assuring reasonableness of schedule and work procedures, and then disappeared for the rest.

Quality and Quantity

If you buy the notion that quality takes time, then it won't come as any surprise to you that there is an inverse relationship between quality and quantity: The higher the quality, the lower the quantity (for the same expenditure of time and money). There are wonderful situations where this relationship does not apply, but usually it does.

This relationship suggests a daring strategy for quality improvement: reduce quantity. Whatever it is that your organization makes, make less of it. Make less and choose much more carefully what it is that you make. The only way you're going to be able to achieve the Adobe Photoshop kind of quality is to strictly curtail your total of new products undertaken by excluding those that don't have a prayer of achieving major impact. Make the ones that matter and put all your resources into them. Take the time and spend the money necessary to do them right.

Reduce quantity? Gulp. I can practically hear you protesting, "Hey, I'm in favor of quality, that's for sure, but we have to put out a given quantity of stuff (all of it high quality, of course)." This is a philosophy first articulated by a world-famous efficiency expert:

> "Quantity has a quality all its own."
> —Vladimir Ilyich Ulyanov (Lenin)

In modern-day business terms, the Leninist dictum comes out this way: "We naturally assume that *all* the products we decide to make are worth making; the only problem now is to make them all to the highest-quality standard."

That sounds good in the abstract, but in the specific, it seldom stands up to examination. Almost any organization I visit (those that work entirely on products for internal use as well as those that develop directly for market consumption) shows me an array of products that varies from the essential to the inconsequential. Cutting out the inconsequential would be, for most of them, the most important act of quality improvement.

The prescription "Make less and choose much more carefully what you make" is a tough one to swallow. The problem is that the "quality" that quantity has is *power.* If you scale back your operation and focus on one or a few great projects, you're still running a scaled-back operation. You're less powerful. You may have fewer people, less space, less total visibility. If the product you choose is a winner, the power will come back, but in the interim, you've lost.

This unfortunate quality/quantity dynamic was at work at Apple Computer under Michael Spindler. The company proliferated products as fast as it could. The consumer was confronted by a baffling array of model numbers and variants. Each one represented a successful little power center within the company. But the company as a whole was going down the tubes. When Steve Jobs arrived back on the scene, he turned the dynamic around and focused all available resources on a much-reduced iMac product set.

Quality Reduction Programs

Quality takes time and reduces quantity, so it makes you, in a sense, less efficient. The efficiency-optimized organization recognizes quality as its enemy. That's why many corporate Quality Programs are really Quality Reduction Programs in disguise.

A common way to make yourself more efficient at the expense of quality is to shift some of your cost to your customer. I think of this as "taking it out of the customer's hide." You see it in airlines when they reduce the cost of meals essentially to zero (you then have to pick up dinner on your own tab), or in hotels where cost reduction leads to ever smaller rooms for the same price. Since so much of the cost of today's business is labor, the ultimate efficiency saving is to transfer to your customer labor that used to be done by your employees. I encountered this in dealing with my company's HMO, NYLCare at the time. The monthly bill came with an extra employee added, someone we'd never heard of. We fired off a complaint and received a letter back from NYLCare, containing the following amazing paragraph:

> We do apologize for the error on the billing. When the application for the client was sent to our corporate office it was sent in with your group number. Apparently the employee put the incorrect number on their application. There is no way to know

when an application is received that it does not belong to the group shown. The office would have to call on every application received and as there are thousands received daily, that would be impossible. The error is being corrected so please deduct the $203.70 from your bill. The credit will show on the next bill.

I particularly like the part "there is no way to know . . . that it does not belong to the group shown." There is, in fact, no way to know without checking. And checking, as the letter points out, can be damned expensive. So the effort of checking was adroitly transferred over to the client. (We should have sent them a bill.)

17

Efficient and/or Effective

THE OVERSTRESSED ORGANIZATION is so busy making itself efficient that it has clean forgotten how to be effective. The two are not at all the same. You're efficient when you do something with minimum waste. And you're effective when you're doing the right something. It's possible to be one without the other: efficient but not effective, or effective but not efficient.

Of course it is also possible to be both. Possible, but not easy. You ought not to be obliged to choose strictly between the two, but suppose you were. Which one would you choose? Efficiency or effectiveness? That's pretty easy. An effective but not efficient organization moves steadily (though maybe not quickly) toward its real goals. How much progress it makes in that direction is a matter of how inefficient it is. An efficient but not effective organization, on the other hand, is moving in the wrong direction. The more it optimizes, the more progress it makes away from its real goals. Such an organization could say of itself, in Yogi Berra's words, "We're lost, but we're making good time."

Why Achieving Both Is Not Easy

Let's face it, the implicit goal in all organizations is to be both: to make effective choices about what to do and then carry those choices out efficiently. That presumption is so strongly built into organizational cultures everywhere that their executives sometimes can't see when it isn't happening. It's absolutely supposed to be happening, so it must be. The fact that the organization *is* moving in a given direction is strong a priori evidence that that must be the *right* direction. They are annoyed when anyone in the organization challenges direction. "We wouldn't be doing this stuff at all if it weren't right; now what we need is for everyone to get on board to help us do it as efficiently as possible."

Unfortunately, momentum in some direction or other does not necessarily imply carefully thought-out strategic thinking. A company can begin to move (or be moved) by a process that is more or less *drift*. The Brownian motion within the company asserts a net force in some direction and "By God we're moving." The difference between strategic thinking and drift is a matter of whether the key choices are made mindfully or mindlessly.

It may sound like a harsh charge that organizations are setting directions mindlessly, that they're prone to get their tactics right but not their strategy. But tactics are a lot easier than strategy. Tactics can be handled in isolation. You as head of a single department in your company can optimize that department to make it more efficient in what it does, but you can't unilaterally redirect it to do something different. That change would have to be effected above you, where the issues are an order of magnitude more complex. And it would have to be done in such a way as to build wide consensus among disparate interest groups. This requires both powerful vision and charismatic leadership. The idea that drift is often substituted for strategic direction-setting is no more surprising than the observation that visionary, charismatic leaders are few and far between.

All this suggests that a lot of companies are not really led at all. If that's true, why isn't it more apparent? Why don't they seem leaderless? That is the direct result of what I call the Easy Executive Option.

> Directing an entire organization is hard. *Seeming* to direct it, on the other hand, is easy. All you have to do is note which way the drift is moving and instruct the organization to go that way.

It was the Easy Executive Option at work, for example, that caused General Motors to cede the small-vehicle sector to foreign competition or to lag behind during the eighties and nineties in energy-efficient engines and nontraditional fuels.

In addition to being flat-out hard to do, building effectiveness into an organization often comes into direct conflict with increasing efficiency. This is an unfortunate side effect of optimization, first noted by the geneticist R. A. Fisher, and now referred to as Fisher's fundamental theorem: "The more highly adapted an organism becomes, the less adaptable it is to any new change." Fisher's example was the giraffe. It is highly adapted to food found up among the tree branches, but so unadaptable to a new situation that it can not even pick up a peanut from the ground at the zoo.

The more optimized an organism (organization) is, the

more likely that the slack necessary to help it become more effective has been eliminated.

Risk Adds Further Complication

The inherent conflict between effectiveness and efficiency is never so evident as when a risky new endeavor is proposed. The nature of risk is that it takes you away from your base of competence and into a new domain where you are effectively an amateur. That's why it's risky.

Because modern market economics are in such flux, companies have to be aggressive risk-takers to succeed. But the efficiency imperative has the direct result of making them risk-averse. Yes, they tell themselves, we could move into this new (and probably promising) area, but only by sacrificing the important improvements we've made in these past years of patient and thoughtful optimization. It's a powerful argument against any risk-taking, often powerful enough to balk the proposed change. Efficiency 1, Effectiveness 0.

But wait. In the opening of this chapter, didn't we agree that if we had to choose between effectiveness and efficiency, we'd choose effectiveness every time? That the alternative makes no sense at all? How, then, is it possible that companies are routinely making exactly the no-sense choice? What on earth would cause them to favor efficient over effective? I'll tell you. It's a management philosophy called Management by Objectives.

18

Management by Objectives

MANAGEMENT BY OBJECTIVES is a fad from the 1950s, now largely discredited. But it hasn't gone away. Badly run companies everywhere are still plagued by this simplistic, easy-as-pie management technique that most often achieves ends that are the exact opposite of those intended and desired. Like most hard-to-shake diseases, this one seems to thrive on the same mix of factors that damages its host. And it is self-perpetuating: MBO companies respond to each failed quarter by instituting still more MBO. Bottom-line failures are excused as due to uncontrollable market factors, while successive improvements in selected quantitatively expressed objectives are loudly touted as proof that management really is succeeding in spite of the dismal results.

MBO Primer

Here's how it works: Performance of each department or division of the company is characterized by one or a few quantitative measures, called objectives. Managers are now encouraged to manage to the objectives, to cause each indicator to move in the desired direction toward its selected target. A manager is declared to have succeeded completely if the objective meets or exceeds the target.

An entire MBO company might have its production department managed to an objective of maximized units off the assembly line, its sales department managed to an objective of increased unit sales, a marketing department managed to an objective of advertising coverage per dollar, a personnel department managed to an objective of minimized dollars of overhead per employee, and so forth.

The underlying premise here is that progress toward the various component objectives assures movement toward the organization's overall goals, presumably profit, growth, and corporate health.

Mired in Stasis

MBO is always based on stasis, the organization's present steady state. MBO sends the message "Do everything the same as last year, only this year do more of X." Setting increased X as the objective is a sign that management has determined that increments of X (assuming nothing else changes) will make their way into the bottom line.

Continuing stasis is a consequence of the first flawed assumption at the heart of MBO: the ingenuous belief that success of the overall organization can be viewed as a simple arithmetic combination of lower-level objectives. The assumption is almost impossible to implement unless nearly everything is in steady state. Without a year or two of experience with current approaches, management has no way to scale the objectives. There is nothing to base a target on. Formulating the "simple arithmetic combination of lower-level objectives" is just too difficult without being able to use a stable model for guidance.

But stasis plus just a bit of tinkering with the particulars is hardly a recipe for success in the new economy. Companies that are succeeding today have very little stasis. For example, the entire concept of "production" is going away. Production implies a steady state. In its place we find a state of almost constant flux. The new central organizing principal is the project. A company in this kind of flux can be viewed as a portfolio of projects. Each project seeks to effect some change.

In an older, simpler time, projects were a way to move from one status quo to another. The project was a disruption, but the new status quo, once established, could be expected to last for an extended period. Now there is no new status quo.

MBO depends on status quo. It assures merely incremental change. It guides you to make tactical adjustments only, always under the limitation that you mustn't muck with the present strategy, whatever it may be. This is a sure path toward extinction.

Dysfunction

The second flawed assumption of MBO is that the net contribution of something as large and complex as a corporate department can be reasonably approximated by a single indicator (or, in a more advanced MBO company, by two or three such indicators).

MBO's objectives are always simplistic approximations. The total meaningful contribution of the few hundred (or few thousand) employees that constitute a typical department is far too complex to quantify. It simply cannot be expressed as a single number. But don't worry about that, MBO tells us, do it anyway.

Come up with the best simple quantification of performance you can, and let that stand for the more complex reality. So X, the selected objective, will stand for C, the organization's total real contribution to the company's ultimate health. We just have to assume that as X improves, C will also improve.

This assumption is the equivalent of what I stated above as the premise that increments of X (assuming nothing else changes) will make their way into the bottom line. The rub here is that something else always changes. For example, a department managed to the objective of increased throughput may drive up its personnel turnover. The net effect of worsened turnover may more than offset the effect of increased throughput. When this happens, X has gone up but C has gone down. This is what Harvard professor Rob Austin calls *dysfunction*.[1]

Austin offers the following classic (perhaps apocryphal) example of dysfunction: The commissars governing a Soviet nail factory decree that henceforth the factory will optimize the number of nails produced. The factory puts out a record number of nails, all of them teensy-weensy little brads. Whoops, dysfunction: Objective was met, but overall well-being declined. Since nobody wants that many brads, the commissars revise the MBO objective. From now on, they decree, the factory will maximize the total *tonnage* of nails produced. Again the factory meets the objective, this time by producing only huge railway spikes. Dysfunction again. The poor Russian carpenter who was hoping for some #10 finished nails is still waiting.

Believers insist that dysfunction is not an intrinsic flaw of MBO, but a simple matter of poor implementation. When dysfunction occurs, they (our era's new commissars) refine and redefine the objectives and try again.

[1]The definitive treatment of dysfunction is in Robert D. Austin's landmark work, *Measuring and Managing Performance in Organizations* (Dorset House, 1996).

After five decades of experience with MBO, its believers are still refining and redefining and still waiting for results. I'm ready to call MBO's constant failure intrinsic. MBO is to an organization what Soviet-style central planning is to an economy: an idea whose time has passed.

Postscript

I am not the first to rail against MBO. The first was, I believe, W. Edwards Deming, famous for his "Fourteen Points" leading to organizational transformation.[2] In point 12 of the Fourteen Points, Deming takes aim at MBO in all its forms. MBO, Deming writes, provides artificial, *extrinsic* motivators—the objectives—which drive out workers' *intrinsic* motivators. So a salesperson, for example, driven by the extrinsic motivator of selling to a quota, will set aside the intrinsic motivator to assure customer satisfaction. The result is likely to be increased sales of marginally needed goods to a narrowing base of increasingly disenchanted customers. Deming's advice on MBO: Get rid of it.

[2]W. Edwards Deming, *Out of the Crisis* (Cambridge: MIT Press, 1982, 1986).

Part Three
Change and Growth

You can't grow if you can't change at all. This may not sound like a revelation to you, but I frequently come across organizations that frankly admit they can't change, that they are stuck in stasis, but nonetheless consider growth a normal expectation. It's a big surprise to them when growth fails to happen. I suspect they treat it as the second of their two big problems: (1) can't change and (2) can't grow. They tend to miss that the second is a direct result of the first.

Even companies with an acknowledged inability to change—that critical absence of slack—can still talk a good game about *flexibility*. They may be in a deep rut and clueless about how to get out of it, but are nonetheless inclined to discuss flexibility as a valuable corporate asset. It's like money in the bank, they seem to be saying, never mentioning that the current balance in that account is zero. They will tell you gamely about the steps they have instituted to improve the f-objective. These steps often include items I have identified as barriers to change, such as reduced slack, standard process, poured-in-concrete processes and voluminous documentation of everything that will hold still for it.

Part Three turns to the subject of making organizational

change—and hence growth—possible. This ambitious task involves more than simply removing barriers to change. It also requires vision, leadership, timing, and a lot more. Slack is the lubricant that makes all these things possible. Vision and leadership, in particular, depend on degrees of freedom made available to the potential visionary or leader. Box these gifted people in tightly enough, and none of their magic will be able to happen.

19

Vision

MY FRIEND Sheila Brady was regaling us one night over dinner at her Woodside, California, home. The rain was coming down in sheets and wind was whipping through the eucalypts and the wine was flowing freely: a perfect time for let-your-hair-down storytelling. Many of the stories were of Sheila's days at Apple, where she was a star project manager. But then the tales turned to Silicon Valley start-ups of more recent vintage, and she opened the floor to the subject of vision. Others around the table (they were employees of half a dozen Valley start-ups) leaped in. They began to talk about vision, mostly observed by its absence.

The most common sign of absent vision was the sense of not knowing "who we are." One particularly depressing example was a top-level meeting at a new Valley dot-com where the company's only apparent reason for existing was to make millionaires out of everybody in the meeting as quickly as possible so they could all retire. Nobody really wanted to be there two years later. Talk at the meeting moved naturally to the success of E-Bay, that month's most astonishing stock market highflier. "Hey, why don't we have some sort of auction component for our company?" one of the engineers proposed. And so they discussed for hours how to work an on-line auction into a company that had nothing to auction and no particular auction skills or capabilities.

"What was missing from that meeting," Sheila observed, "was someone who was willing to say, 'Auction might be nice, but it *just isn't us.*' "

It's nontrivial for a company and everyone in it to know "who we are." A little bit easier, however, is to know "who we aren't." When even that knowledge is missing—when there is no basis in the company to say about a given cockamamy scheme "it just isn't us"—the company clearly lacks vision.

Vision implies a visionary. There has to be one person who knows in his or her bones what's "us" and what isn't. And it can't be faked. Employees can smell an absence of vision the way a dog can smell fear.

Vision and Change

Vision is the sine qua non of constructive change. Without vision, a company can react, but it can't pro-act. It can lay off workers or close plants or retrench. Those are changes, in a sense, but they aren't Change; they don't deliver the much-vaunted benefit we're supposed to get from whatever flexibility we manage to build into the organization.

Without vision, flexibility is just an abstraction. It is a measure of what we could do if we ever got the gumption to try it (but we haven't and we won't).

Successful change can only come in the context of a clear understanding of what may never change, what the organization stands for. This is what Peter Drucker calls the organization's *culture*. Culture, as he uses the term, is that which cannot, will not, and must not change. We talk a lot about changing corporate culture, as though it were just another parameter of the organization, like an SIC code or address. But Drucker would have us look at culture entirely differently, as the bedrock upon which any constructive change will have to rest.

If nothing is declared unchangeable, then the organization will resist *all* change. When there is no defining vision, the only way the organization can define itself is its stasis. Like the human creature that fights wildly to resist changing whatever it considers its identity, the corporate organism without vision will hold on to stasis as its only meaningful definition of self.

The Visionary Statement

A visionary statement is a strong assertion of "who we are." Consider an example: an American president engaging his people with the statement "Ask not what your country can do for you; ask what you can do for your country."

The statement looks like a challenge, but it's much more than that. The "ask not" statement is a call to action that depends for its force on an unspoken ending: Ask what you can do for your country *because this is what we are all about*. Without that unspoken ending, the challenge falls flat. The assertion at the heart of the quoted visionary statement is that the community lend-a-hand ethic is so deeply entrenched in this culture as to be positively definitional.

The successful visionary statement will typically have the following characteristics:

1. There has to be an element of *present* truth to the assertion. The challenge "Run a four-minute mile *because that's what we are all about*" would not inspire most of us because we wouldn't see the present truth of the "what we're all about" part.

2. There is always an element of proposed *future* truth in the statement. Though it masquerades as "what we *are* all about," it is at least partly urging us toward "what we *could be* all about."

3. When the statement walks perfectly between what is and what could be, and the could-be part is wonderful but not impossible, acceptance by those listening is almost assured.

People want to sign on. They want to be enrolled. Nobody listening to the president that day had the reaction "Oh damn, now I have to do stuff for my country." On the contrary, they were delighted. The emergence of a leader is a source of satisfaction and completion for all. People want to be led toward a vision that is consistent with reality and their present assessment of the culture. When an organization is in drift and then suddenly everyone is aware that a hand has taken the helm, the sense of relief is palpable.

The fact that people want to be led is what makes leadership possible at all.

20

Leadership and "Leadership"

THERE'S LEADERSHIP, and then there's "leadership." The first conveys vision, engenders confidence, and encourages striving toward common goals. The other doesn't.

Chances are you've encountered some of the inside-quotemarks kind of leadership in your own career, but just in case not, I offer the following example. In September 1989, President George Bush and governors of the fifty states convened a National Education Summit at the University of Virginia at Charlottesville. In his address to the group, the president thundered that American youth would be "number one in science and math by the year 2000." He repeated this assertion in his State of the Union Address on January 31, 1990. And then . . . nothing. That was it. Just that vehement statement and vehement repetition that American students would be best in science and math. (I guess it was up to someone else to take it from there.)

The context of Mr. Bush's statement was that American students had recently performed dismally, finishing in the lower third on math and science test results among Western societies. So the president had to take things in hand and show us the way. As I write these words, we are midway through the year 2000, and guess what? American students are not first in math and science. Not even close. In fact, they're still performing dismally, at about the level they were in 1989. This is an object lesson on where "leadership" can get you.

In a sad footnote to the above, President Bush later observed that the United States "has the will but not the wallet" for education reform. The truth is exactly the opposite: The country had the wallet (in spades) but not the will. Creating the will was his job.

What Is Leadership Anyway?

Leadership is the ability to enroll other people in your agenda. Meaningful acts of leadership usually cause people to accept some short-term pain (extra cost or effort, delayed gratification) in order to increase the long-term benefit. We need leadership for this, because we all tend to be short-term thinkers.

There is no easy formula for real leadership (if there were, we'd see a lot more of it), but it seems clear that the following elements always need to be present:

1. Clear articulation of a direction
2. Frank admission of the short-term pain
3. Follow-up
4. Follow-up
5. Follow-up

When we're presented with the first of these and none of the others, it's not leadership at all. It's just "leadership," nothing more than posturing.

Since I began with an example of hollow posturing, let me now contrast that to a real act of leadership. The Finnish company Nokia up until the end of the fifties was a successful wood pulp and paper company with a few new acquisitions in low-tech areas such as transmission cable. In 1960, two engineers from Nokia Cable Works formed a grand vision of a new Nokia, one with both feet in high tech and no feet in paper and pulp. The Nokia of today is pretty much what Björn Westerlund and Kurt Wikstedt had envisioned in 1960. How did it happen?

If you had been there, you would be able to cite a few early things that mattered: a blueprint developed by Westerlund with the help of a handful of academics and outsiders, formation of an electronics department under Wikstedt to begin implementing items from the blueprint, a diffident but at least tolerant attitude from above. From that point on, though, the picture gets fuzzy. How did everyone get enrolled, particularly executives from the paper side? How was the present truth of Nokia's identity (as of 1960) used to lead toward the vision of "what we *could be* all about"? How did the necessary skills get built? How were investors cajoled into supporting this change of direction?

It's not easy to say how any of these things happened because there was no one single act to enable any one of them. There was instead a broad spectrum of measures at all levels to make sure that everyone got enrolled and stayed enrolled. This kind of leadership is an ambitious *orchestration* of direction and encouragement. It became every manager's business at Nokia from the 1960s on. It still is. In such a context, a manager who is 40 percent used up making operations happen is not viewed as 60 percent reclaimable expense. Rather, he/she is viewed as someone doing leadership 60 percent of the time. If there is an incentive to change this formula, it suggests looking for ways to

decrease the time spent running operations to free up more capacity for leading the transformation.

The Question of Power

When attempted leadership fails, there is always one ready excuse: not enough power. This was essentially what President
Bush was getting at when he said his country didn't have the
wallet. The missing "wallet," as he saw it, was the extra incre-
ment of power that he needed to be able to lead toward better
education. If it had been available, he seemed to be saying,
then he would surely have succeeded.

Lack of power is a great *excuse* for failure, but sufficient
power is never a necessary condition of leadership. There is
never sufficient power. In fact, it is success in the absence of
sufficient power that defines leadership. The little acts of leadership you encounter every day are often performed by relatively powerless people, or by people whose capacity to enroll
others far transcends their power to force compliance. After
all, what does *enroll* mean if, as boss, you can instead *oblige* people to do whatever you tell them to do?

Think of your own experience, not leading, but being led:
Have you ever taken direction from someone who didn't have the
authority to make you obey? Of course you have. And how do you
feel about that? How do you feel about the person who led you?
Chances are, the more that person was operating successfully outside and beyond his/her designated authority, the more strongly
you feel that you were lucky to have been touched by a real leader.

Lines of Hierarchy and Lines of Leadership

Leadership is not restricted to acting only downward along the
lines of organizational authority. The bread-and-butter acts of

leadership that make companies healthy involve people leading their bosses, leading their peers, leading those in peer organizations, negotiating, mediating, and influencing, all without ever being granted the official power to do what they're doing.

It's enrolling someone who is distinctly outside the scope of your official power base that constitutes real leadership.

21

Dilbert Reconsidered

IF YOU'RE COMFORTABLE with the idea of leadership working up the organization chart and sideways across the white space, then the obligations of being a subordinate are changed for you forever. Everyone, even the person at the very bottom of the hierarchy, has some potential to lead. And having the potential implies some obligation to use it.

Potshot at an American Hero

Not so many years ago I would have told you that Dilbert was one of my great heroes. Today I would tell you that Scott Adams, Dilbert's creator, is one of my heroes. Adams gives insight and wisdom on nearly a daily basis and serves it up with a delightful twist of humor. What a marvelous body of work he has created!

Adams is a hero, but Dilbert himself—the geeky guy with the pointed-up necktie—is no hero. Dilbert is a jerk. He keeps his head down, doesn't object to even the most absurd of corporate absurdities, never makes waves, never puts his job on the line. It's Dilbert and his ilk who make stupid management possible. If you've got people like that working for you, you start each management day at a disadvantage.

It's a rare company I visit these days that doesn't have a Dilbert cartoon posted somewhere. I guess the message of these cartoons is "Our company is in some ways like Dilbert's company," or, even worse, "My boss is in some ways like Dilbert's boss." When I encounter these cartoons, I always want to find the person who posted them and ask, "Yes, but are you like Dilbert?" Are you keeping your head down? Are you accepting senseless direction when it's offered? Are you letting the bureaucracy dominate at the expense of the real goals? If so, I'd like to tell that person, then you're part of the problem.

At the risk of being a total killjoy, I propose that you look at the next Dilbert cartoon that falls under your eye in a totally different way. I propose that you ask yourself about Dilbert's role in whatever corporate nonsense is the butt of the joke. Ask yourself, How should Dilbert have responded? (The real Dilbert, of course, never responds at all.) How could Dilbert have made this funny situation distinctly nonfunny? What could he have done to put an end to such absurdities? There is always an obvious answer. Sometimes the action is one that would get Dilbert fired.

It's easy (and fair) to blame lousy management on lousy managers. But it's not enough. It's also necessary to blame the people who allow themselves to be managed so badly. At least partly at fault for every bad management move is some gutless Dilbert who allows it to happen.

Who Then Shall Lead? (How About You?)

Thirty-five years of public speaking have taught me this: The more successful I am at persuading a business audience of the need to make some difficult change, the more likely people are to come up to me afterward and say, "I wish my boss could have been here to hear you say that!" I must have received that comment three hundred times or more over my career.

At first I thought these comments were a sign that my message was coming into the organization at the wrong level. I urged my agents to change their marketing approaches, to find me an audience that was situated higher up on the org chart. To my surprise, these higher-level managers made the same comment. They, too, had bosses, after all, and they, too, wished their bosses could have been there to take on the required change. Well, who wouldn't? Wherever you're placed in the chart (except, I guess, in the catbird seat), you have a boss, and your boss has more power than you do. If the change really is a difficult one, what a relief if he or she could make it happen instead of you.

After all these years of hearing "the comment," it now provokes in me an entirely different response. When people tell me, "I wish my boss could have been here," I know my message has landed and I've gotten it to exactly the right person. If the message had made no sense to the receiver, he/she would have wandered away without comment; if the message conveyed no call to action to that person, there would have been nothing to resist. The person who is wishing most fervently to thrust the responsibility onto some higher-up is the very person who knows that he or she *could* make the change happen, but of course it won't be easy. It will involve managing upward and sideways, and perhaps calling in some markers from people all around the organization. An act of leadership is about to happen.

Followership

My personal favorite among those cloying "corporate impressions" images that are sold through the airlines magazines is a picture of a pack of horses (viewed from behind) charging along in a cloud of dust. The caption is L•E•A•D•E•R•S•H•I•P, but what the image really conveys to me is "followership." After all, most of what you see is nose-to-tail followers.

Similarly, when I listen to executives wax loquacious on the importance of leadership, I'm often impressed that the real message they're conveying has more to do with followership than leadership. They're trying to instill an ethic of follower-ship in the organization. The leader, as they see it, is an elite, and the great mass of (unwashed) workers is supposed to fol-low that elite. The problem with an ethic of followership is that it makes leading the exclusive domain of the anointed elite.

The most exciting companies I know have no ethic of fol-lowership at all. By that I mean that people sometimes follow, but they are not *innate* followers. In such companies, leader-ship is everybody's business, and following someone who's got the inspiration of the moment is also everybody's business. Leadership is a rotating function. Following whoever has got the hot hand is a side effect.

22

Fear and Safety

Sticks and stones can break my bones,
but names can never hurt me.

I WAS TAUGHT that saying before I was five; you probably were too. The version I've quoted is in English, but a saying conveying that same idea occurs in virtually every language. In this chapter, I will ask you to reexamine the idea underlying the saying and (perhaps) come away with an entirely different conclusion.

Sine Qua Non of Change

The single must-be-present ingredient of successful organizational change is safety. (Again, my catchphrase "successful organizational change" means proactive change, not reactive change.) Since people define themselves—in part at least—by what they do professionally, changing what they do gets deep into the matter of personal definition. This is scary stuff.

Resistance to this kind of change can be fierce. It can also be hidden, angry, vituperative, and destructive. Against all this, managerial coercion is simply no match. You can't *make* proactive change happen; the best you can do is *help* it to happen. In place of coercion, your only workable tool is urging.

Change always implies abandonment. What you're abandoning is an old way of doing things. You're abandoning it *because* it's old, because time has made it no longer the best way. But it is also (again because it's old) a familiar way. And more important, it is an approach that people have mastered. So the change you are urging upon your people requires them to abandon their mastery of the familiar, and to become novices once again, to become rank beginners at something with self-definitional importance.

People can make this kind of change, but they can only make it if they feel safe. In an unsafe environment, people are not likely to let themselves be thrust into a position of inexperience. They will resist the change, and all your urging won't shake them from their determination to have no part of it.

Fear (Reexamined)

When you're not safe, you feel afraid. And fear can inhibit change. Interestingly, though, fear does not *always* inhibit change. People sometimes manage to effect great change in themselves when they're scared to death. Some of these changes are purely reactive (brought on by the fear), but some aren't. Some kinds of learning are enhanced by fear. If that weren't true, ice climbers and sky divers and oil well firefighters would never be able to learn their skills.

When your thirteen-year-old son skateboards up onto a cement park bench and off the other side and turns a flip in midair on the way down, your parental concern may make you ask, "Weren't you afraid you'd break your neck?" The answer comes back, "Aw, Mom, of course not!" Which means yes. Of course he was afraid. Skateboarding is apparently one of those skills that are best learned with a healthy dollop of fear.

Learning, the key activity of meaningful change, is not antithetical to fear. I will go so far as to suggest (in Chapter 26 just ahead) that fear is a constant in any kind of essential learning. So if fear is not a fatal deterrent to learning, why is safety so important for change? And what does safety mean anyway, beyond a simple absence of fear?

Rather than consider these questions in the abstract, let's concoct some specifics: Imagine that you are a new hire in a brand-new e-company that has set out to make an electronic marketplace for trading currency futures. If you've got your head screwed on right, you have taken this job with trepidation. Neither you nor anyone else really knows what it means to trade currency futures in a newly created electronic market. There are plenty of reasons to doubt your future: Suppose some competitor beats you to the punch; suppose the market is so thin that bid/asked spreads are unworkable; suppose the Mafia slips in to take advantage of a security lapse; suppose regulators impose multimillion-dollar bonds and your company can't raise the funds; suppose the investors get impatient; suppose the burst traffic is too high for the hardware; suppose a day's trades are lost due to some kind of failure. Most of all, suppose the company just fails for these or any other reasons and you are out on the street, forty-nine years old and jobless. Erghhh.

So you're afraid. You'd be crazy not to be. Can you make changes in the way you do your day's work? Of course you can. Companies like this exist on change; they *are* change. Everybody in them is scared, but everybody can still change.

Paradoxically, the fear of breaking your neck (translation in corporate terms: losing your job) does not make change impossible. It's a much more insidious kind of fear that interferes with change: the fear of mockery. If you want to make change in your organization utterly *impossible,* try mocking people as they struggle with the new, unfamiliar ways you have just urged upon them. There is no surer way to stop essential change dead.

The safety that is required for essential change is a sure sense that no one will be mocked, demeaned, or belittled while struggling to achieve renewed mastery.

Sticks and Stones and Names

So sticks and stones in the world of corporate change are survivable, but "names" are killers. Irony and sarcasm, pointed jabbing criticism, personal mockery, public humiliation, exasperation, managerial tantrums, eye-rolling: These are the true enemies of essential change. To make an organization change-receptive, you need to rout all of these various kinds of disrespect from the culture. Replace them with a clearly felt sense that people at all levels are to be honored for the struggle they've been willing to take on.

During change, every failure has to feel like a treasure (for the lessons it imparts). The person who fails is a hero, the backbone of the change effort. Failure gains that person more respect, not less.

Make this one essential change to your organization in order to make any other change possible.

23

Trust and Trustworthiness

A COMMON FEATURE of the stock market page is the story of a company that has recently turned a corner. They seem to come up with a new one almost every week. A year before, the company seemed to be in full-fledged drift, leaderless and headed for oblivion. And today there is someone clearly in charge, prospects are looking better, and the stock is moving up. What on earth happened in between?

Somehow a leader emerged. He/she was hired in from the outside or promoted from within, anointed by a board of directors or retiring CEO (whoever does the anointing at that company), and then . . . and then what? My answer is that the new potential leader went through some initiative period and came out of that period with widespread trust. Without this gaining of trust, there is no leader, and no real turnaround. But how is trust gained, and how does it ever happen so swiftly?

How Trust Is Gained: The Default Model

Before getting on to the business of how a new leader really does acquire trust, we need to first reexamine our preconception about gained trust, the one that was planted in our firmware by parents and teachers during our formative years. Those parents and teachers wanted to show us how to gain their trust. But—let's face it—they had an additional item on their agendas as well: They wanted us to behave. The model they gave us is therefore all about *deserved* trust. They didn't tell us about *undeserved* trust, because their agendas would not have been well served by describing an alternative trust-gaining mechanism. The omission was a fair one given their objectives, but it leaves a key gap in our understanding of how leadership emerges. It leaves us believing this:

You gain trust by demonstrating trustworthiness.

That's it. That's the only way to gain trust (or so they implied).

Like many of our firmware rules, this one looks a bit odd when reduced to black and white. Just how are you supposed to demonstrate trustworthiness without having something entrusted to you to demonstrate upon? Whatever that something is, it has to be entrusted to you beforehand, and therefore well before you really deserve it. The truth is that there is no possibility of achieving trustworthiness except through the mechanism of *undeserved trust.*

All the time that our mentors were impressing upon us the necessity of demonstrating trustworthiness before trust is conferred, they were advancing us little dibs and dabs of totally undeserved (not-yet-deserved) trust for us to work on. The basic rule they were impressing upon us was quite at odds with the rule that they themselves were learning as part of their own increasing mastery of child-rearing. What they were learning was this:

Parents' Rule:	Always give trust slightly *in advance of* demonstrated trustworthiness.

How a New Leader Gains Trust: The Real Model

The emerging leader simply doesn't have time to gain trust by demonstrating trustworthiness, even if that were possible. The only path to success is to acquire not-yet-deserved trust. So, if you are the brand-new CEO of Hewlett-Packard, for example, you find yourself empowered not so much by the sober judgment of those below ("I conclude that the new boss has proved herself worthy to be followed"), but by their collective hunch ("I'll bet she's gonna be a winner!").

I've been lucky enough in my consulting work to watch a few highly successful emergers in action. They have all been master trust gatherers. Watching them has convinced me that picking up not-yet-deserved trust requires substantial personal magnetism. The people who do it best tend to be articulate, colorful, attractive, wry (I'm thinking of one CEO with a huge ego, but also a delicious self-deprecating humor).

Those are innate characteristics: Either you've got them or you haven't. More interesting, therefore, are the *mechanics* of acquiring not-yet-deserved trust. Here I see one pattern common to all the winners. The one mechanical practice they all have in common is this: *They acquire trust by giving trust.*

Leadership and the Giving of Trust

Arriving in Sydney one morning after an endless night flight from L.A., I waited for the crowd to pass before standing up into the aisle. One other person who had decided to wait was a mother with her two little girls, a few rows ahead of me. Since I had only one shoulder bag on that flight, I paused beside her and asked if I could help with some of her gear (it's always amazing to me how much stuff mothers need to carry with them). "I've got an arm free," I said. "Could I carry something for you?"

"You sure could," the woman answered. And she plunked an angelic little blond-haired girl into my arm. I went off the flight as high as a kite. The mother had brought along a two-kid stroller, which she unfolded just inside the terminal. I put the little girl into her side of the stroller and said good-bye. The entire incident took up three minutes of my life and it was nineteen years ago. But I haven't forgotten it and I never will.

The giving of trust is an enormously powerful gesture. The recipient gives back loyalty as an almost autonomous response. Gifted leaders know in their bones how to entrust. It is something they do on a daily basis. They give responsibility well before it's been completely earned. They know when to turn their backs and take their chances.

As a young engineer, I was privileged to work under a succession of great managers at Bell Telephone Laboratories, Computer Applications, La CEGOS Informatique, and Swedish Philips. Beside each of those managers' names I could write down a specific act of undeserved trust, a responsibility they assigned to me just slightly before the rest of the world (even I myself) would have been ready to acknowledge I had earned it. Even today I feel emotional about some of those assignments. At the time, I was proud and delighted, and also scared stiff. Most of all I was determined that the person who had so trusted me would not ever regret it.

I've written about the giving of trust as though it were a simple formula for building loyalty. But it isn't simple at all. The talent that is an essential ingredient of leadership tells the leader whom to trust and how much to trust and when to trust. The rule is (as with children) that trust be given slightly in advance of demonstrated trustworthiness. But not too much in advance. You have to have an unerring sense of how much the person is ready for. Setting people up for failure doesn't make them loyal to you; you have to set them up for success.

Each time you give trust in advance of demonstrated performance, you flirt with danger. If you're risk-averse, you won't do it. And that's a shame, because the most effective way to gain the trust and loyalty of those beneath you is to give the same in equal measure.

24

Timing of Change

To every thing,
Turn, turn, turn,
There is a season,
Turn, turn, turn,
And a time to every purpose under heaven.
　　—The Byrds (with help from Ecclesiastes)

I F TURNING (changing) the organization is your particular charge, you're going to need a market timer's sense of the right and the wrong moment. Doing the "right" thing at the wrong time is worse than taking no action at all.

Just to complicate the matter, conventional wisdom on timing a change tends to give you a shove in exactly the wrong direction. Conventional wisdom tells you, "If it ain't broke, don't fix it." In other words, only consider changing anything when it clearly *is* "broke." That leads to the situation shown in the graph on the next page.

You can't pour change freely into the corporate equation (the way you can with an extra bonus or benefit) anytime it might be handy. There are times when change simply won't take. And, conversely, there are opportune moments when an organization is reasonably disposed to accept change.

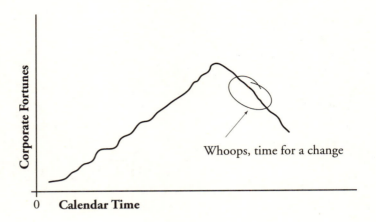

Whoops, time for a change

Change: What You're Up Against

You, as a corporate change agent, probably have no strong commitment to the current way of doing business, but that doesn't mean that no one else does. After all, once the change is successfully made, you're likely to wander off to change something else, while those whose world you've just thrown into turmoil are going to have to stick around and live with the results. As long as people tend to define themselves at least partially in terms of the work they do, any change to that work, its procedures and modes, is likely to have self-definitional importance to them. This can lead to surprising amounts of change resistance.

Let me put this into perspective: You're David, and the change resistance you're likely to encounter, to even the most innocent-seeming change, is Goliath. You're a puny little human and Goliath is a giant, six cubits tall. (For purposes of this discussion, assume that 1 cubit = 1 mile.) Of course, in the story, David did slay Goliath, but remember that David had heavenly support. Unless there is some reason to believe that God is on your side and personally committed to your organization's transformation, then the rest of us are going to be inclined to bet on Goliath.

You clearly need some serious advantages working for you

to be able to overcome this level of resistance. Among the advantages are (1) a set of sensible approaches to change introduction and (2) a culture that is not change-phobic. Rather than offer specific advice in these two categories, I'm going to refer you instead to a book about change introduction[1] and one about corporate culture[2] and concentrate here on the third advantage you'll require: (3) proper timing.

The Goliath-like resistance to change is not exactly logical; it's much more likely to be emotional. How people feel can be more a factor in the success of a change than what they think. Anxiety of any kind can only complicate the task of change introduction. That's why the period of sudden decline of corporate fortunes is exactly the worst moment to introduce a change. People are uneasy about their jobs, worried about lasting corporate health, perhaps shocked by the vitality of the competition.

In retrospect, a far better time to introduce the change would have been back in the period of healthy growth.

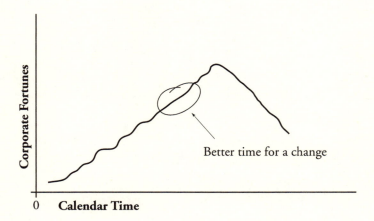

[1]W. Bridges, *Managing Transitions: Making the Most of Change* (Addison-Wesley, 1991).

[2]T. DeMarco and T. R. Lister, *Peopleware: Productive Project and Teams* (Dorset House, 1999).

Growth always carries with it a certain *necessity* for change. You may have to hire more people, expand to larger quarters, diversify or centralize, all to accommodate your own burgeoning success. But growth feels good; it feels like winning. It even feels good enough to reduce the amount of change resistance. Since growth is winning, people look at growth-related change entirely differently.

Change on the Rising Tide

Growth is the rising tide that floats all boats. The period of growth is one in which people are naturally less change-resistant. It is therefore the optimal time to introduce *any* change. Specifically, changes that are not growth-related should be timed to occur during growth periods. This is not because they are strictly necessary then, but because they are more likely to be possible then. You need that advantage going up against Goliath.

25

What Middle Management Is There For

THIS CHAPTER turns temporarily from the overall question "How does change happen?" to focus on a narrower matter: *Where* does change happen?" Specifically, where in the organization is the change center?

An easy (but wrong) answer is that change happens at the top. The incentive for change may well come from the very top, but not the specifics of change. Change, particularly a significant one, involves reinvention. And corporate reinvention requires a deep involvement in the day-to-day business of the organization, something that top management is no longer likely to have.

An equally wrong answer is that change happens at the bottom. People at the bottom of the hierarchy just don't have the perspective to reinvent, nor do they have the power to carry out any reinvention scheme.

If reinvention doesn't happen at the top and it doesn't happen at the bottom, there is only one possibility remaining: It's got to happen in the middle.

The Key Role of Middle Management

The key role of middle management is reinvention. Oh yes, middle managers are also responsible for directing operations and other ongoing activities. But the distinction between companies that survive the turmoil of our changing economies and those that don't is middle management in its change agent role. The survivors will have vital, confident middle management, particularly at levels 2 to 4. The nonsurvivors will be the ones who trimmed those midlevel positions to the bone during the nineties, and so terrified and disenchanted the middle managers still left that they no longer have the gumption to act.

Let me restate this idea even more brutally: The companies who today find themselves stuck in stasis are that way because they fired the very people who were capable of helping them get through necessary change. They flattened themselves by getting rid of their change centers. (Here I mean the word "flattened" in both of its senses.)

Part of the flattening logic had to do with identifying midlevel people with time on their hands and getting rid of them. This was called trimming fat. The fact that they had time on their hands made them fat.

Bringing Back Slack

If the essential task of middle managers is reinvention, when is that task to be carried out? The answer is, during time that is not used up directing the day-to-day business. The fact that managers have time on their hands (i.e., their operations tasks use up less than eight hours per day) gives them time for reinvention. The extra time is not waste but slack. Without it they could function in only their operational roles. Reinvention would be impossible because the people who could make it happen are just too busy to take the time.

Even companies that didn't fire their change centers have hurt themselves by encouraging their middle managers to stay extremely busy. In order to enable change, companies have to learn that keeping managers busy is a blunder. If you have busy managers working under you, they are an indictment of your vision and your capacity to transform that vision into reality. Cut them some slack.

Isolation

Sufficient slack is not the only necessary ingredient for reinvention. Middle-level managers need to work *together* to conceive of and make any meaningful change happen. And middle managers almost never work together. In fact, managers at all levels tend to work in relative isolation.

Even first-time managers, brand-new at the task, might find themselves sitting alone in a closed office, wondering how their peers would deal with some of the problems they've just been handed. You might think they'd buttonhole some older manager and say, "Hey, however did you deal with [whatever]?"

That certainly would be sensible, but it's not so easy. The comfortable, shared involvement and collaboration that is common among nonmanagerial knowledge workers is less common among managers. In its place is an uneasy tension, a sense of competitiveness. That competitive tension is particularly evident when middle managers don't feel safe. They are all thinking that if somebody has to go, let it be one of the others. This is hardly an attitude to foster collaboration.

Safety Again

I stressed earlier that the people who will be asked to bear the brunt of the change have to feel safe. This applies equally well to the people who conceive of the change and direct its implementation. Change can't happen without risk, and risk-taking is only possible in an environment that can be tolerant of at least some failure. There is a paradox at work here: Making it okay to take risks and succeed in risky endeavors requires that you also make it okay to fail.

If you're having trouble with the notion that risk-taking requires tolerance for failure, consider the opposite: punishment for failure. Potential punishment is often justified as a way to assure success; it is more often a deterrent to taking any risks at all.

Summary: The Requisites of Reinvention

Reinvention takes place in the middle of the organization, so the first requisite is that there has to be a middle. I'll assume your organization still has one. Now pour in some slack, increase safety, and take steps to break down managerial isolation. Voilà, the formula for middle-of-the-hierarchy reinvention. (Sounds easy until you try to apply it.)

In order to understand why each of these elements is necessary and how to make them happen, we need to look into the core activity of reinvention, which is organizational learning, the subject of the next chapter.

26

Where Learning Happens

I SUPPOSE you could change an organization without ever learning anything, but what would be the point? It's usually something you've learned that motivates the change and a set of new skills you learn along the way that effects the change. Learning and change go hand in hand.

The Human Learning Machine

People are natural learning machines, learning all the time. Evolution built this learning facility into us and *didn't provide a switch*. So, for example, when you lay aside your First World War history book in the evening—thinking, "Well, that's enough learning for one night"—and enter into a conversation with your spouse or your kid, *learning doesn't stop*. It just switches gears. Learning never stops till you're dead.

Organizations, too, are learning all the time. But it doesn't always take, and not all of it is useful. To become an effective *learning organization*, you need to make a habit of learning those particular skills and directions that become the genesis of constructive change. This is considerably less natural. In (maddening) fact, we tend to sop up new knowledge like sponges when the thing we're learning is largely irrelevant to us, and resist learning things that really matter. This is true for organizations and also true for individuals. You, for example, may have no trouble learning something about a war that happened nearly a hundred years ago, but might find yourself at least partially blocked when it comes to mastering a drastically different way to do your job.

Classical Model of the Learning Process

Educators tell us that the learning process consists of four elements: learner, facilitator (sorry about the teacherspeak), material, and co-learner(s). The model looks something like this:

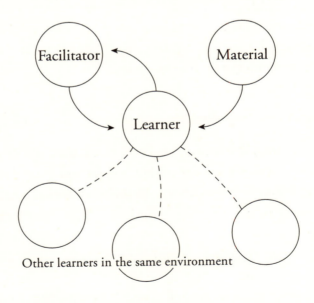

The learning environment: classical education model

Clearly, some learning can happen in the absence of one or more of these elements. Think of yourself alone with that history book: no facilitator and no co-learners. We learn all the time in such a partial learning environment. But remember, it's not the easy, natural learning of the nonprofessional that is the subject here, but the learning of those things that really matter, that change the way we do essential, self-definitional work. And for that kind of learning, the full environment is almost a necessity.

An example: Let's say that your World War I history book teaches you that the battle called Chemin des Dames in 1918 was complicated by the mutiny of a Russian army on loan to the French. (The pro-revolution soldiers were rebelling against their czarist officers.) As an amateur historian, you can learn this little fact easily and go on. But suppose that you are not an amateur. Suppose you are a *professional* historian. Suppose that you had written a book yourself about Chemin des Dames and had never heard till this very moment about the Russian mutiny. This is an entirely different matter. What you are being encouraged to learn has significance to your self-image. You really ought to put yourself back immediately into basic research mode, track the subject down, and either publish a retraction of your own work on the battle or lodge a protest against the mutiny theory. That way you will learn and grow. You ought to do that, but there is a contrary tendency at work within you as well. The contrary tendency is to dismiss the whole idea of the mutiny as preposterous and never think about it again: An opportunity to learn something important has just been lost.

White-Faced Learning

I know from my early years of teaching development methods that when people learn something that really matters to them, they go through a moment of panic. As soon as it's apparent that this new approach is superior to what they have been doing for years, there is an unspoken "Oh shit" that ripples through the room. Their faces turn white. You can practically hear the flip-flops in their stomachs.

At such a moment, it helps the learner to be able to glance over at someone else whose face is also white, who's also got a little perspiration showing on the upper lip. The presence of the co-learner, the patient urging of the facilitator, and a lot of easy, unthreatening reinforcing material are necessary to help get people past this professional's learning block. Without all these elements in place, many or all of the potential learners will dismiss the troubling new idea as "preposterous."

Why Teams Matter

Teams of knowledge workers are something of a puzzle. Almost all the real work undertaken by the team ends up being done by individuals working apart, little done in true team mode. Why, then, is the team so important? Why do well-jelled teams of knowledge workers perform so much better than nonteams?

Part of the reason is that the team helps align goals, helps to keep all members pulling in the same direction. It also satisfies some of the individual's need for community. These are nontrivial advantages that go a long way to explaining the demonstrated advantages of teamwork in knowledge activities.

Now add to this the elaborate learning environment that the team supplies. When you learn within the context of a team, you have a facilitator: another team member who is advanced somewhat ahead of you in the subject. This is your coach. You have material: a comfortably doable piece of project work that has been carved off for you by your coach to help you master the skill. And you have co-learners: the other team members who are learning at the same time, or who have just been through the experience themselves (and whose faces are still pale). This is a perfect environment for learning what really matters. This is probably the context of most of what you learned early on about your profession.

The team provides an ideal learning environment, a place where coaching and being coached are an integral part of each day's work.

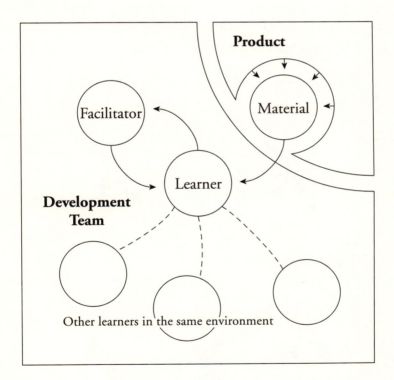

The idea that teams matter to learning may seem like good news for your organization, since chances are it is highly supportive of teams. That's fine, but where are those teams? It's not uncommon to see real teams as a phenomenon of only the bottom level of the hierarchy. When that's true, you have to wonder: Are we set up to learn only at the bottom level? Do we have teams where learning really matters?

Learning How to Manage

Companies need to learn a lot of different things, but the most essential of these is management. Nonmanagers are promoted all the time; lower-level managers are promoted up to tasks where the management skills required are qualitatively different. How do they learn? Sadly, they are most often obliged to learn in a depleted learning environment.

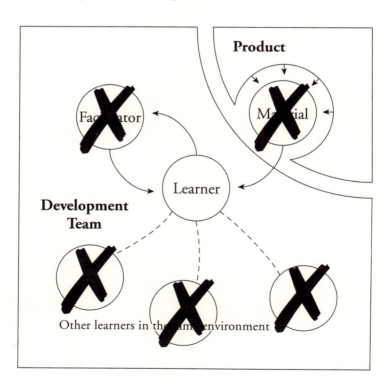

Here we see no coach, no peer facilitator. There is no material, other than the whole job, no easy, unthreatening piece carved off to provide an ideal learning exercise. And there are no evident co-learners. The new manager is expected to learn whatever needs to be learned in almost complete isolation.

In my own case, as a young manager I was alone inside a closed office. I had access to my boss, but not to the people who really could have helped, the other managers at my own level. Each new management challenge I faced caused me to wonder, How on earth would Sharon or George or Eugene (my peer managers) deal with such a problem? I'd have killed for the opportunity to be a fly on the wall of one of their offices, just to be able to watch an expert at work. There was a complex and ugly set of rules in that culture that made it impossible for managers to ask each other for help.

Oh yes, young managers are often supplied a bit of management training. The problem with such training is that it's all abstraction and no example. It is no replacement for the context of the team where you learned your earlier skills by actually applying them to pieces of real work. While we're at it, management training tends to teach only the mechanics of management (reporting, running the scheduling system, Gantt charting, PERT analysis), and none of the really difficult things that distinguish good managers from bad: people selection and motivation, team jelling, listening, promoting, choosing correctly when to entrust new responsibility.

Most of us don't learn well from abstraction. We learn from example. That's part of the reason why we don't learn well in isolation. The skills of management—like the skills of parenting—are best learned by example and with the help of able coaching and shared experience of peer learners.

Why can't new managers learn their skills in the context of

a team? After all, there is something that is at least *called* a management team at virtually every company.

The Management Team

Part of my first day on a new consult is usually spent with the management team. I find myself in a room with a dozen or so other people, taking part in a weekly status meeting. All these meetings are pretty much of a kind. The boss makes a few comments and then subordinate managers take turns telling the boss what's happening in each of their areas of responsibility. When Manager D is speaking his piece, you might see Manager G, a bit farther down the table, making a few notes. I've come to suspect that the notes almost never have anything to do with what others are saying at the meeting; rather, Manager G is making notes for her own few minutes of addressing the boss. Managers who have already had their moment in the sun affect a passive listening posture that is very close to asleep. When the managers stand up and exit the room, they will not typically see each other till the next status meeting.

The status meeting I've portrayed is not really a meeting at all; it's a ceremony. At a real meeting, n people put their heads together to arrive at some conclusion or to take some new direction that requires the input and participation of all. Taking turns talking to the boss is not a meeting in this sense. It is, rather, a ritual that acknowledges and celebrates the bossness of the boss. There is need for ritual in business, I guess, but let's at least understand that the weekly status meeting is not really a meeting.

And the management team is not really a team. A team is a group of people who have joint responsibility for—and joint ownership of—one or more work products. People who own nothing in common may be called a team, but they aren't. This is not to say that companies never form real management teams, only that they do so rarely. Most of what are called management teams are a mockery of the team concept.

When you find a real management team in action, there are a handful of managers who run their respective subgroups together. People in the subgroups are aware that their bosses are spending a lot of time with each other. (Sometimes they even complain about this: Their past experience has accustomed them to a manager who is alone in his/her office for much of the day, and therefore more available to them.) Decisions are made by the team and belong to the team. Responsibility and accountability are spread over the management team, just as they are in the lower-echelon teams that work for them.

This modest diffusing of accountability is the "problem" cited by organizations that allow no real management teams. They trumpet the advantages of having each manager entirely responsible for whatever is allocated to him/her. The flip side of this simplistic accountability scheme is managerial isolation.

Keep Your Eye on the White Space

In the previous chapter, I asked the question "Where does change take place?" I suggested that since organizational learn-

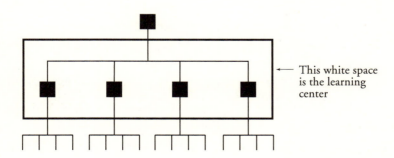

This white space
is the learning
center

ing and change are so closely allied, your change center would turn out to be your learning center. And I further suggested that all transformational change and learning take place in the middle of the hierarchy. But where in the middle? My precise answer is that change and learning take place in the *white space* at the middle of the org chart.

Significant organizational learning can't happen in isolation. It always involves the joint participation of a set of middle managers. This requires that they actually talk to each other and listen to each other, rather than just taking turns talking to and listening to a common boss.

Companies that are best at organizational learning have vital, communicative white space. This is true all up and down the hierarchy, but particularly at the middle. The white space between peer middle managers is where reinvention happens. If the white space is not conducive of communication and joint responsibility, reinvention doesn't happen at all.

27

Danger in the White Space

THIS CHAPTER looks at the opposite side of the coin from the last one and focuses explicitly on the *nonlearning organization*.

When companies and divisions and departments get themselves totally stuck, when they can't learn their way out of a paper bag, they often look to change the lines and boxes on the org chart. They'd be better off to concentrate on the space between those lines and boxes. Since healthy organizations use this white space as their learning center, you can bet that the nonlearners have got trouble exactly in the white space. Instead of being vital and collaborative, their white space is isolating and dangerous to explore.

An upsetting example of the problem was described by an attendee at one of my seminars when he told me over lunch, "I'm *afraid* of my peer managers." He went on to say that at his company, managers were pitted against one another. He was made to feel that another manager's success was his own failure and that, conversely, the other managers' failures were good news to him. Of course the others felt the same way—that's why he feared them. They were always looking for a chance to undermine his strengths or exploit his weaknesses.

Where there is such "danger in the white space," organizational learning—along with all other forms of cooperation and collaboration—grinds to a halt.[1]

"I Guess a Little Healthy Competition Won't Hurt Them"

As often as you find organizations characterized by intense competition between peer managers, you'll find someone a bit higher up on the hierarchy who will make you think the tension is put there by design. "I guess a little healthy competition won't hurt them," he or she will tell you. Over the years, I have come to believe that this kind of competition is almost never explicitly designed into an organization; rather, it happens without anyone really wanting it. And the manager who excuses it (who almost seems to be taking credit for it) is a sad example of the self-deluding authoritarian who assumes that anything that happens must necessarily have been exactly what he/she intended to happen.

It's interesting to speculate on how the competition does arise. When siblings are competitive, it's often a result of being undernourished in some sense, feeling deprived of attention, affection, feedback, or approval. Maybe competition among peer managers and the danger in their white space are due to the same sort of undernourishment. Maybe it is the ungiving,

[1]It was my friend and Atlantic Systems Guild colleague Suzanne Robertson who coined the deliciously dramatic phrase "danger in the white space" to describe the problem of learning-inhibited companies.

strict authoritarian nature of some upper managers that engenders competition, or at least lets it happen.

Internal Competition Exacts a Price

There is no such thing as "healthy" competition within a knowledge organization; all internal competition is destructive. The nature of our work is that it cannot be done by any single person in isolation. Knowledge work is by definition collaborative. The necessary collaboration is not limited to the insides of lowest-level teams; there has to be collaboration as well between teams and between and among the organizations the teams belong to.

In all fairness, managers who allow and encourage competition among their subordinates have not missed the need for cooperation among those very same subordinates. But they have persuaded themselves that competition won't inhibit cooperation. They reason that the obligations of "professionalism" will oblige their subordinate managers to help each other out when it is in the common good. When that doesn't happen, they grumble about "unprofessional" behavior.

This notion of professionalism strikes me as hysterically optimistic. When managers are given direct and explicit incentives to compete with their peers, it makes no sense to expect them to refrain from playing the game at all out of respect for a fuzzy abstraction like professionalism. And for all our preaching on the subject, professionalism is most often just a fuzzy abstraction. What, after all, does it mean to manage a department professionally? Is one to be guided by a professional ethic intrinsic to management per se or one intrinsic to the particular kind of work that department does (research, or claims processing, or public relations)? In any event, competition is not inherently unprofessional. It wouldn't be unprofessional to compete to win against a rival company in the arena of the marketplace. It might not be a great idea under some circumstances: for example, in wartime, when you and your rival are both part of the war effort. We all take guidance from the managers above us as to where to direct our competitive energies; if that management steers us to compete directly with our peers, it can hardly complain that we've acted unprofessionally in doing so.

Playing Defense

Any vigorous competition will entail at least two elements: offense and defense. Offense is the effort you put into scoring against your opponents, and defense is the effort you apply to stop them from scoring against you. Those who suggest that "a little healthy competition can't hurt" are thinking only of the offense part. They reason that "scoring," whatever that means in context, can be aligned through clever management to something that is beneficial to the organization as a whole. That way when the individual connects, the organization is also a winner. It is possible, I suppose, to align winning for the individual with winning for the organization, but it is never easy. This kind of alignment comes perilously close to Management by Objectives and is thus subject to all of MBO's failings, in particular dysfunction. When dysfunction happens, the individual scores and the organization comes out the loser.

The offense component of internal competition is problematic, but the defense component is always injurious. When peer managers play defense against each other (try to stop each other from scoring), they are engaging in anticooperation.

Instead of encouraging competition and then depending

on abstract notions like professionalism to discourage a natural inclination to play defense, companies have to learn to rout out competition between managers. Danger in the white space might help an organization to be efficient, but it will never allow it to become effective.

There's a Pattern Here

Competition happens under authoritarian managers. Slackless organizations tend to be authoritarian. When efficiency is the principal goal, decision making can't be distributed. It has to be in the hands of one person (or a few), with everyone else taking direction without question and acting quickly to carry out orders. This is a fine formula for getting a lot done, but a dismal way to encourage reinvention and learning. The people who could do the reinvention are unempowered, and they're too damn busy anyway to reinvent anything.

Learning and reinvention take time. If people are too busy doing the work, they will never have the time to learn new ways to approach it. Authoritarian management is obsessed with time. It is destructive of slack and inclined to goad people into outperforming their peers. And it makes learning impossible. Which brings us to the matter of training . . .

Training

I know, I know, this section should have gone in the previous chapter ("Where Learning Happens"), not this one, which is about nonlearning. In fact, you're probably wondering, What's the matter with this DeMarco guy anyway, not having a section on training in that chapter? Isn't training the way that organizations learn?

My point in placing it here is that training, as normally conducted in the slackless organization, is a nonlearning technique.

Before making that point explicitly, let me describe to you an ideal training situation, one that is highly likely to result in learning. Imagine that you are a beginning piano player, just showing up for your first lesson. Ms. Melodie, your teacher, tells you that you're going to begin by working on the Malagueña Suite. "Whoa," you respond, "I have only these ten fingers." You wiggle them helpfully to make the point. "No way I am going to be able to play Malagueña." "That's okay," she tells you, "we're going to take it extremely slowly." And so you begin. She has you play the first phrase at one-tenth the speed that a concert pianist would play it. And then you go back over it again and again till you've got your fingers pretty much trained, not to "play the piano," but to play that one phrase. Then you move on to the next.

My point is that the essence of a training experience is this slowing down. (Learning takes time.) It is the very defining characteristic of training.

Training = practice by doing a new task *much more slowly* than an
            expert would do it

Any so-called training experience that lacks the slow-down characteristic is an exercise in nonlearning.

Most corporate training fits easily into this category. You are given an input-only stage in which you ingest some new idea or approach, and then a performance stage in which you practice it. Only you don't get to practice it at a tenth the speed (or even nine-tenths the speed) that an expert would do it. Rather, you are expected to practice at expert speed. Armed with the new (untried) technique, you are supposed to do the same work you did the old way in less time than it used to take you. That, the training department will tell you, is the reason you were trained in the new technique: so you could be more efficient.

Chances are you've been guilty of "training" people this way yourself. Have you ever assigned a new (first-time) manager to a project and allocated about the same time for him or her to bring the project home that it would have taken had you run it yourself? I've done that. If I could have managed the project myself in a year, I would expect the first-time manager to have it done in a year as well. I don't know what I thought I was doing, but it sure wasn't training. If I'd wanted to train that manager, I should have given him/her twenty-four months or more to do the job. I should have insisted that the project be run with fewer people than I'd have assigned to it had I been the project manager. With fewer people on board, the new manager would have an easier time grasping the lessons offered up by the experience.

There is no training without an extended period of practicing at a much slower-than-expert rate. In today's Hurry Up corporation, that usually means there is no training. Real training is starkly at odds with Hurry Up. And the Hurry Up message is everywhere; it pervades the organization like wallpaper.

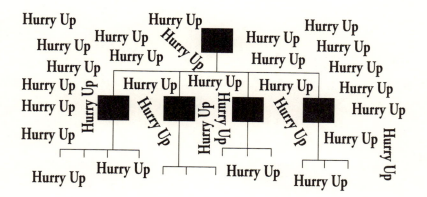

This, too, can be viewed as a problem of the white space: It's too dangerous to navigate and too full of the Hurry Up message to serve for the communication of anything else.

Rx for Nonlearning

To transform a nonlearning organization into one that at least can learn requires two simple changes:

1. Drive internal competition out of the organization to enable cooperation, collaboration, and joint ownership among managers.

2. Take time for the practice stages of training by allowing people to exercise their new skills at a much slower-than-expert rate.

What's simple about these transformations is stating them. A bit more complicated is the task of making them happen.

28

Change Management

THE TERM "change management" has always struck me as almost touchingly optimistic. It suggests that you manage change pretty much the way you manage the mail room or the Southwest Regional Office. Would that it were so!

The sense in which you "manage" change is more nearly akin to the management in that other optimistic term, "cancer management." By this I don't mean to imply that change is undesirable, only that it is uncertain of outcome and almost impossible to steer. It has its own course to run, and all your efforts to affect that course may have influence, but can never really be thought of as controlling. That's not the fatal limitation that it may at first seem to be: Influence in the hands of a talented manager can accomplish more than full control in the hands of someone who is talent-free.

Suppose you really do manage the mail room during the workday and then during the late daylight hours most spring days, you manage the local Little League baseball team. What are the differences between these two kinds of "management"? Well, during the day you can tell people once what to do and they pretty much do it. On the ball field, you have to say everything again and again to get the message heard. You have to remonstrate, repeat, correct, encourage, cajole, and motivate. Whatever you're doing, you may have to start it over from scratch a few times. Your charges don't always listen, they seldom obey; they seem a million miles away while you try to get their attention, and the next kid up to bat may be off in the woods taking a leak. This is the kind of management that change managers are good at.

The Rules Are Different

Many of the rules that we take for granted in our normal management activities are different in the midst of change. Included among these is what I think of as the Cardinal Rule of Management: I am boss and you are not, so do what I tell you to do. Even managers who are not at all authoritarian benefit from this rule; it's always there, hanging in the air. For example, if you judge your own manager to be particularly reasonable and disinclined to rely on authority, it's only because he/she has got some authority not to use. The Cardinal Rule is always at work in management situations . . . except in change management.

When a full-fledged change is in progress, it's almost impossible to tell the difference between someone who's diligently trying and failing (normal mode during change) and someone who is rejecting the change. Since *you* can't tell, the people you manage don't ever have to come to grips with whether they're failing or just not taking part. The Cardinal Rule is effectively suspended. You can rail against that, but you might better accept it. In the absence of normal authority, you'll need to rely on your powers of persuasion and your abilities to lead without positional power. Your role is, for the moment, less that of boss and more that of negotiator.

The Game Is Over Before It's Begun

Another key way in which management is different during times of change is that the assumption of Reward After Performance has broken down. Reward After Performance is so much a part of the corporate world that you may not even be aware of it, but it's always there. You receive a paycheck *after* you work for some period, not before. There is always the tacit understanding that should you not do the work, perhaps the pay won't be there either. Similarly, the various kinds of soft compensation—praise, enhanced responsibility, esteem of co-workers—all come after performance.

In times of change, the reward has to come first. Another way to say this is that the basic currency that pays for change is the set of "markers" you can call in for favors done and confidence earned in the past. Great change managers have got a lot of markers to call in. They have built a reservoir of trust and they tap into it to entice their people to embrace change.

This is bad news for the new guy on the job who comes in as a stranger to organize and command a change. He has no markers to call in, nothing really to work with except a little "honeymoon capital." It's never enough to promise people that benefits coming at some later date will make the change all seem worthwhile. The harsh reality confronting this new manager is that the key activity of change management (the building of trust) had to be done before the change was even given a name.

The Factory/Family Model

By the time we arrived on the scene for our first day of work, we already had a tentative model of how the manager/worker relationship would look. This model was based on our experience within the family. Dad was boss. The kids were supposed to take orders—they didn't always, but they were always supposed to, and when they didn't, there were sometimes "consequences." Without any other idea of how things ought to work, we assumed the job would function in much the same way: boss = dad, and worker = kid.

This model is also a common one in factories. Many of us who manage knowledge workers today are children of fathers who were factory managers in their day (my dad ran brass and bronze foundries in the New England states). So when our fathers came home with work stories, the stories confirmed that management on the factory floor was pretty similar to management within the family. There was authority, direct orders, obedience, and "consequences."

The factory/family model of management just isn't applicable during periods of change. Some of the key rules are different, as I've set out above. But here I want to make a slightly larger point: The factory/family model—even in times of stasis—doesn't apply very well to the management of knowledge workers. That's because stasis in a knowledge organization is a relative term; it just means a time of somewhat lessened variability. The key tools of management in the knowledge organization are the tools of change management. Instead of authority and consequence (the management staples of the factory floor), the best knowledge-work managers are known for their powers of persuasion, negotiation, markers to call in, and their large reserves of accumulated trust.

Part Four
Risk and Risk Management

Sea change in our global economy has brought us new modes of doing business, new markets, and borderless competition. All of this spells out opportunity, and opportunity implies risk. Nobody is going to succeed without taking chances and we all know it. Risk-taking has come to be recognized as a modern necessity. Even the most staid of today's corporations know that risk is something they dare not run away from.

An appealing definition of success in such an environment is this: *Take lots of risks and overcome each and every one of them.* When the specifics of all these little triumphs are entered into the official plan, the result is an approach called Plan for Success. Plan for Success is a staple of management philosophy, particularly in our high-tech industries. It leads us to pour desired outcomes into concrete, and make commitments based on achieving those outcomes.

Plan for Success is the intellectual equivalent of: Make big bucks by winning fifteen consecutive hands of blackjack without taking any money off the table till the end. It works when it works, but leaves you in the lurch when it doesn't (which is most of the time). It also puts an effective damper on risk-taking. An organization that is expected to overcome *all* adversity can't afford to take on any but the most trivial risks. Conversely, an organization that has suffered no important setbacks has in fact taken no real risks.

Risk management is almost the opposite of Plan for Success. Risk management is—take a deep gulp of air here, this is going to be unsettling—a discipline of *planning for failure*. Companies that practice risk management make explicit provision for lots of small (but expensive) failures along the way to overall success. Overall success means taking a lot of money off the table at the end.

Taking a risk means exposing yourself to additional cost or delay. If you take lots of risks, some will end up costing you and others won't. You may catch a break on the whole: Say only one in ten of the bad stuff that might have happened actually does happen and actually costs you extra time or money. But you can't count on dodging all risk consequences. You need to set aside some slack of time and money to accommodate a likely break on risks that materialize as opposed to those that evaporate. The science of risk management guides you as to how much slack to provide.

29

Uncommon Sense

THE FORMAL DISCIPLINE of risk management is as old as the insurance industry. Since it was developed by and for insurers, let's begin by examining the idea in its original insurance context.

If you are an executive of Lloyd's of London or Aetna or John Hancock or GEICO, you will tend to think of risk management at the portfolio level. Your risks are not well managed if too many of your portfolio holdings (policies) are subject to loss due to the same catastrophic event. So, for example, too heavy a concentration of coastal Florida property policies exposes you to boom or bust: If there is no hurricane, you coin money, but if there is a hurricane, you may be wiped out entirely. What could you do to spread out this risk? What step could you take to assure that your downside is acceptable without forgoing all of your upside benefit (all those lovely premium checks rolling in from clients)?

The prototypical insurance risk management action is to lay off some of the risk to another insurer, typically in exchange for one of that insurer's own unbalanced portfolios of risks. You exchange some of your Florida property coverage for part of another company's California disability coverage, or Hawaii workers' comp, or key man insurance in Silicon Alley. Now if a hurricane strikes the Florida coast, you incur losses, but not so great as to bankrupt your company.

Note the following from our insurance example:

1. Risks are not inherently bad. (Risks are the entire reason there is money to be made in your business.)

2. Risks don't ever go entirely away. (You still have some loss when the bad thing happens.)

3. Managing the risk costs you something (the work of laying off the extra policies and the penalty your partner companies may impose upon you before accepting some of your too-risky coverage).

4. If the risk doesn't materialize, risk management costs you something extra (the lost profit of all those property premiums in a year when there were no loss claims).

5. The discipline is applied to the entire portfolio, not to any one of its constituent risks. (Having all your eggs in one basket—only one policy—gives you no way to assure that that policy won't incur claims during the year.)

All these things are true of risk management in the insurance business and will also be true of risk management in your business.

The Bad News

Since you're not an insurance executive, your principal use of risk management will probably be to manage a single risky endeavor, say a project. If so, you do have all your eggs in one basket: that project. You understand that the role allocated to you is to succeed at that project because *the company is counting on it!* The bad news is that risk management does not give you a way to force the success of that project, only to maximize the odds of its success. If enough of the project's component risks actually materialize, the entire effort may fail—that is, it may fail to complete on time, it may overspend its budget, it may not be able to deliver enough value by the deadline.

The control that risk management gives you is stochastic, not deterministic. You have *deterministic* control, for example, over the pressure of a given weight of gas in a vat; how you set the temperature and alter the volume will determine the pressure absolutely. As long as you get to set these parameters, you are totally in control. You have *stochastic* control over the rate at which employees leave your company to take jobs with the competition. Variables like salary and benefits and work hours and pressure have a tendency to affect the leave-rate, but no matter how correctly you set them, there is no guarantee that Harold will stick it out till the project ends.

Stochastic control may be fine for the company, but not so good for an individual manager who comes up a winner or a loser based on a single undertaking. But it's important to realize that *it is good for the company.* Furthermore, some projects are large enough to be considered complete portfolios of risks, and it may be possible to use stochastic control within the project to achieve overall success.

Added to the bad news of no deterministic control is more bad news that the tools of risk management are more than a little counterintuitive. Since they deal with uncertainty, they are of necessity probabilistic in nature, hence not so easy to grasp. Finally, a last bit of bad news: A risk management approach is distinctly at odds with an article of corporate theology called

Can Do Management. (More about Can Do at the end of this chapter.)

I've presented the negatives of risk management up front. All the rest is good news. But the negatives make quite a devastating package: nondeterministic control, counterintuitive tools, and misfit with an important part of corporate culture. Why on earth would you want to do such a thing?

Why You Want to Do Risk Management Anyway

Suppose I came into your company to work with your key project for a few days. Suppose at the end of my stay I informed you that "the project has no chance at all of being completed before the end of May; my best bet is that it will be done September 1. Of course the worst-case scenario is a lot grimmer, say middle to end of next year."

You knew you were uncertain about the project's likely delivery date before you called me in. I make no bones about being uncertain either. The difference between your uncertainty and mine is that I have given you some information about precisely *how* uncertain I am. I can see possible delivery happening anytime over the range from June 1 to next December. I have

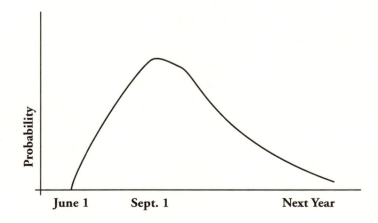

furthermore told you something about where the delivery likelihood peaks, my *best bet* of when the project will be done. In
graphic form, my assessment is represented by the graph on
the bottom of the previous page.

This *risk diagram* is an explicit declaration of uncertainty. It shows
the relative likelihood that completion will happen at any given
time. The area under the graph between any two dates represents
the likelihood that the project will complete during that period.

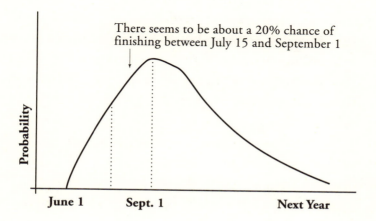

The scale is set so that the area under the entire graph is
equal to one, the equivalent of a statement that there is a 100
percent likelihood that the project will be completed sometime
between the most optimistic and the most pessimistic dates.

Risk management (the simple definition) is the explicit
declaration of uncertainty. It allows you to go forth into risky
territory with some assurance of just how much risk you're running. Explicit declaration of component uncertainties—the
ones that lead to possible late delivery, for example—allow you
to manage a sensible risk reserve across your whole set of risks
to maximize the chances of overall success.

That may seem almost trivial, but consider how projects
may proceed in the absence of explicit risk declaration:

ABUSE: The statement that a project has "no chance at all of being completed before the end of May" will be interpreted to mean that June 1 is a sensible completion date. This results in selecting a date that (as the graph shows) has 0 percent chance of being met.

ABUSE: Certain more liberal managers will set the date at whatever is identified as the "most likely date," but still find themselves finishing late almost two-thirds of the time. The diagram shows why this is: Projects, like most human endeavors, are characterized by long trail-off toward the right, so that the peak of the curve is squeezed left; the area to the left of the peak is barely a third of the total:

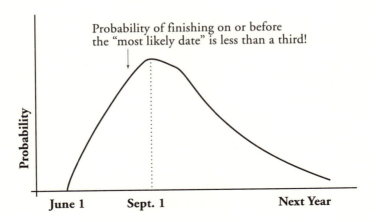

ABUSE: The news that the project may drag on into next year is concealed from clients and stakeholders. When this happens on one project after another, the stakeholders lose faith in all assurances about dates.

My clients often speak of the difficulty of squaring with their stakeholders: "I just can't tell Marketing that their new product might not be ready for another nine months; they'd skin me alive, or they just wouldn't fund the project." But stakeholders are not an amorphous abstraction; they are people—very savvy people with long memories. When they learn that assurances about dates are empty posturing, they have no way to know what real risks they're running. That forces them to be much more conservative, imagining the worst. The paradox here is that organizations *can't be aggressive about risk-taking without some meaningful assessment of the extent of the uncertainties.* Without sensible risk management, organizations are prone to become stubbornly risk-averse.

Facing Up to Uncertainty

Risk management is the explicit quantitative declaration of uncertainty. But in some corporate cultures, people aren't *allowed* to be uncertain. They're allowed to be wrong, but they can't be uncertain. They are obliged to look their bosses and clients in the face and lie rather than show uncertainty about outcomes. Uncertainty is for wimps.

I don't have an easy answer for you if you live in such a culture. Certainly, public risk management is not going to be possible. You might still practice some risk management in private in your own domain—just because you're obliged to lie to your boss is no reason to lie to yourself—but the benefits will be less than if it were able to become a common practice throughout the organization.

A variation on the "uncertainty is for wimps" theme is the culture where managers are allowed to show a little bit, but not a lot, of uncertainty. The amount of declarable uncertainty is typically on the order of 5 percent. So if a project is expected to finish in eighteen months, a manager might get away with insisting on a two-month window, promising completion sometime from the beginning of month 18 till the end of month 19. But that's it—that's the maximum extent of uncertainty allowed. All that would be fine if the company had a strong record showing that it regularly predicted results within 5 percent of actual. Most of the companies I know that have the 5 percent maximum uncertainty rule built into their corporate culture are far less successful at predicting than that. They regularly achieve results that deviate from prediction by 50 to 100 percent. With that kind of track record, insisting on a 5 percent maximum uncertainty window just makes liars out of everyone.

Can Do

Staring your boss in the face and saying June 1 when you know that even a year from June would be optimistic sounds bad. It sounds like lying. But being a Can Do manager sounds good. We're all expected to have a certain Can Do attitude. Admit it: You feel a little thrill of approval when the big boss calls for extraordinary performance and his/her subordinates respond, "Can do." This is the throwing-down and the accepting of a challenge. And accepting challenge is neat. You tell yourself, "Nobody would ever do anything ambitious if they didn't commit to it, no matter how undoable it sounds at the beginning." Can Do thinking is a fixture in most modern companies.

Can Do is, unfortunately, antithetical to risk management. Risk management has to acknowledge directly the Can't Do possibilities. There is no way to be a complete Can Do manager and also practice risk management.

You can't do both yourself, but there is no reason why your company couldn't. The individual manager has to be Can Do or Can't Do in attitude; the two don't mix. The company, on the other hand, could have a mix of complete Can Do managers and a few Can't Do's. The charter for most of you would be to psych yourselves up for success. "But," the boss would explain at the beginning, "Lillian is our Can't Do specialist, our risk manager. It's her job to focus on the uglies, all the could-go-wrongs that might interfere with our plans. All the rest of you succeed if you achieve your most ambitious goals. And Lillian succeeds if she warns me of every possible eventuality that might reasonably be expected to thwart us. She fails if I get blindsided by anything she hasn't warned me about."

30

Risk Management: The Minimal Prescription

A RISK is a bad thing that might happen or might not (or it might happen to some degree). It's bad because should it happen, your chances of overall success are lessened. When the bad thing happens, the risk is said to materialize.

My simple definition of risk management was explicit declaration of uncertainty about the effect that expected materializations may have, and that is certainly the key element. But in addition there is a bit of homework to be done for each identified uncertainty. Work you need to do on a per-risk basis is the subject of this chapter. There are two classes of risk that are handled somewhat differently: aggregate and component.

Aggregate and Component Risks

Aggregate risks are the potential overall failures of any undertaking. If you set out to build a bridge, for example, the aggregate risks are things like these:

❏ You might fail utterly to span the river and have to give up in disgrace.

❏ You might succeed but only at exorbitant cost (a lot more than your investors agreed to pay).

❏ You might get the bridge built eventually, but so late that lost income wiped out all potential profit.

❏ You might neglect certain safety rules and thus cause the deaths of one or more of your workers.

❏ You might put the bridge in place on time and on budget but be disgraced later by its collapse under non-extraordinary circumstances.

When an aggregate risk actually happens, the entire venture is invalidated; you'd have been better off not to have undertaken it in the first place.

The reason you do risk management is to reduce or eliminate the possibility of these overall failures, but it doesn't follow from that that you can expect to manage aggregate risk directly. The essential business of risk management is managing the *component* or causal risks—that is, the set of things that can go wrong that might lead to aggregate failure. For example, inadequate technology or poor engineering are two component risks that could contribute to the aggregate failure to span the river. They are potential root causes of overall failure.

What It Means to Manage Risk

The practice of risk management varies from one organization to another. Some make the process formal, while others practice it almost casually as an integral part of the larger business of managing. No matter what your style, there are certain essentials. You can't claim to be managing your risks unless you:

1. List and count each risk.

2. Have an ongoing process for discovering new risks.

3. Quantify each one as to its potential impact and likelihood.

4. Designate a transition indicator for each one that will tell you (early, I hope) that the risk is beginning to materialize.

5. Set down in advance what your plan will be to cope with each risk should it begin to materialize.

Finally, you will need to create some sort of model that shows how the sum effect of the component risks establishes your uncertainty about overall success. Such uncertainty is typically shown in risk diagrams such as the ones included in the previous chapter. There are usually separate diagrams for cost and schedule, and possibly other kinds of risk.

Risk management needs to be dynamic. By that I mean that the overall declared uncertainty has to be updated over time. Each time a component risk does materialize or fails to materialize (and can no longer come back to bite you), the aggregate risk diagrams need to be updated.

Risk Containment

How you deal with a risk when it materializes depends on its nature, the extent of its likely damage to your prospects of success, and its likelihood.

In the simplest case, you simply take its impact on the chin, pay for it, and move on. The payment may be in the form of money and/or time. Example: You hoped your test engineer wouldn't leave to take another job, but she does. You bring in an expensive replacement, pay all the attendant hiring and training costs, and then watch as your project limps along for several weeks while the new person gets acclimated. Total cost: $35,000 plus a month of probably unrecoverable delay.

Where do that money and time come from? It may look like the money is scrounged and the time is negotiated, but in order for this to happen, there had to be some flexibility built into the budget and schedule. This flexibility is what I shall call a *reserve*.

When bad things happen without warning, we have to scurry around to get the resources to offset them. When such bad things are anticipated in advance through the mechanism of risk management, there is typically an explicit reserve set aside to pay for them. There is not a reserve for each risk, but one for the whole endeavor. The goal is to place in reserve enough time and money to give at least a fifty-fifty assurance that there will be enough to cover the costs of those risks that do materialize. If your uncertainty about cost looks like this:

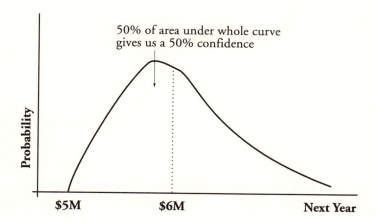

then a risk reserve to give a 50 percent confidence level would be $1 million over and above the minimum budget of $5 million. (You would expect to have a similar risk diagram for schedule and use it similarly to determine the risk reserve of calendar time.)

The risk reserve is money and time budgeted for work that *may not need to be performed!* Without risk management, such reserves would be trimmed in order to come up with a more acceptable budget and price. That is how we so often end up with a budget and schedule that assume no risk will ever materialize (i.e., the 0 percent likely case). Since risk management forces an explicit declaration of uncertainty, it's not a big additional step to budget for some reasonable expectation of risks to materialize.

Setting aside a risk reserve with a 50 percent or better confidence level is called *risk containment*. When risks are paid for out of this reserve, they are said to be contained. It's not a major intellectual effort to know how much time and money are needed to contain the most common risks of our work (half a dozen carefully performed project postmortems supply most of the data). The major effort is to keep the risk reserve from being eliminated by someone who wants desperately to hear lower numbers.

Risk Mitigation

Risk mitigation is the set of actions you will take to reduce the impact of a risk should it materialize. There are two not-immediately-obvious aspects to risk mitigation:

❏ The plan has to precede materialization.
❏ Some of the mitigation activities must also precede materialization.

I shall deal with these in reverse order, since the second is part of the reason for the first.

Consider the risk of fire in a school. As long as it's only a risk—a bad thing that may or may not happen—you don't actually *have* to do anything about it. But when it materializes, the risk changes from merely an abstraction to a real-life crisis. Now you have to act. But if you haven't done work in advance to prepare, some of the actions you most desperately want to take now are not going to be possible. You'd love to have a fire extinguisher, but nobody did the preparatory work of procuring, charging, and placing fire extinguishers. You need a bell to warn the children, but none was installed. You'd like to have the children perform a perfect fire drill exit, but no one has taught them how to do it.

Since some pre-materialization work may be needed to make effective mitigation possible, there has to be a plan in place just to know what mitigation is called for and what preparation it will require.

In the case of the school fire, you certainly knew before I came along that advance work would be needed. What's not so obvious is that mitigation of business risks usually requires advance work as well. It may be intellectually clear, but there is a disturbing tendency to ignore such pre-materialization work because it violates an unwritten rule: Don't do work that might not have to be done. We see this in particular when people are under pressure. (And who isn't?) Give a manager a tight enough deadline and he/she reasons, "Well, I'm going to have to catch a break or two along the way to be finished on time." Because the schedule is so aggressive, catching those "breaks" becomes an integral part of the plan. On the Plan for Success schedule, there is no time for work that might not have to be done at all, that, we tell ourselves, *won't* have to be done because the breaks we're planning to catch will make such work unnecessary.

The minimum pre-materialization work for each risk is to sketch out a plan of what to do if the risk happens. Remember that these planned mitigation activities may eventually end up on the critical path, and pay attention that all their precedence requirements will be satisfied if that should happen.

31

Working at Breakneck Speed

THE HURRY UP MANTRA tells us to do everything as fast as possible. Okay, so how fast is possible? How quickly could you do a given task? You have to imagine yourself working furiously, precisely on track, and with no additional stops to pull out. You're maxed, your mental pedal is to the metal. This is the fastest the human knowledge worker can go. If we were talking about physical progress instead of intellectual progress, this rate would be dubbed "breakneck speed." The Hurry Up mantra is instructing us to do knowledge work at breakneck speed.

Now, where do you suppose the term "breakneck speed" came from? Why do we call it that? That's an easy one. At such a rate, you are positively courting disaster. You're holding nothing back. (If you were, then there would be some additional speed possible, so you would speed up and then you'd be holding nothing back.) Your speed puts you on the brink of a disastrous spill and all its attendant consequences. One minor misstep and all is lost. Hmmm. Does that sound like risk management to you?

The Dirty Little Secret

Proceeding at breakneck speed is, by definition, inconsistent with risk management. Of course you already knew that. But its corollary may have eluded you. The corollary is that managing your risks requires that you go at some slower speed. And the result is that you will finish later than you would have if you had sustained breakneck speed and been lucky enough not to break your neck.

Let's take an example. Suppose you undertake a project with only one significant risk. There is a bad thing that might happen, and depending on whether or not it happens and when and to what extent, it could cause delay on your project. If the bad thing doesn't happen at all, you will finish in twelve months. If it does happen, it could result in putting off project completion by as much as a year. Your most likely scenario is that it will probably cost you a four-month delay.

Here is the risk diagram for the project as I have described it:

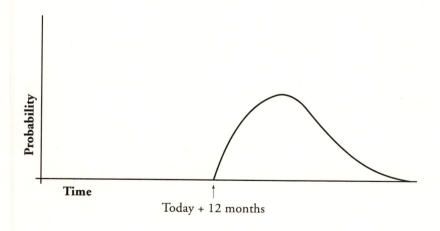

You put your risk management hat on and your first thought is this: What could I do to improve my handling of the bad thing if it does happen? You hit upon a short course to teach some of your key project people how to deal more efficiently with the matter. This is risk mitigation. You realized that the course could cost you a few person-months, but potentially save you a doubling of total cost and save more than half of your potential delay, so you go ahead and send your people to the course. The following diagram shows how your risk diagram changes with mitigation:

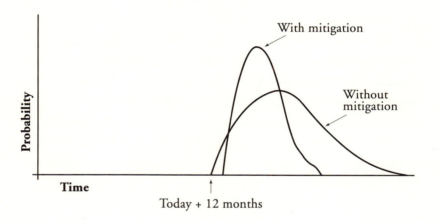

This is a considerable improvement. Your most likely date is moved in by a full six weeks. Your mean expected date (fifty-fifty chance) is moved in by even more. Your worst case is barely half the delay of what you would have had without mitigation. That's the good news.

The bad news is that your most optimistic possibility has worsened. Your rosy scenario is a little less rosy. Without mitigation, you had a snowball-in-hell chance of finishing in twelve months plus a day; with mitigation, your absolute minimum time to finish is increased by the time spent training your workers. This is the cost of mitigation.

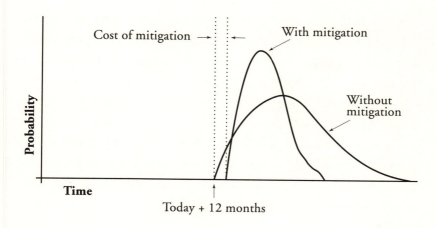

In at least half the companies I visit, people can't focus on any date except the rosy-scenario date. For these companies, risk mitigation makes no sense at all. They can't see beyond the time lost to mitigation. They're planning for success, and risk management just gets in the way.

Mitigation is the jewel in the crown of risk management. If you can't do mitigation (can't take action now to make future risk-containing action possible or reduce its cost), you can't do risk management.

All Prudent Speed

Back in the time of sailing ships, going anywhere by ship was a risky business. Going faster increased risk (more sail kept aloft in high winds, more chances taken in unknown and shoal waters, more fatigue and more human error). In such a time, the naval forces would instruct their captains to "proceed with all prudent speed" to arrive in a timely manner at an engagement. Prudent speed is something other than breakneck speed. It's slower. We have to learn to move our knowledge endeavors "at all prudent speed."

The key to this is to look at entire risk diagrams, not just the rosy-scenario point where they intersect the axis. If a given strategy moves the weight of your risk diagram markedly to the left, then it is a good strategy. Do whatever it tells you to do. If the risk subsequently doesn't materialize, you will have spent some extra time along the way that turned out not to be necessary. Put that in the same category as the money you spent last year on life insurance that turned out not to be needed.

The difference between the time it takes you to arrive at "all prudent speed" and time it would take you at "breakneck speed" is your slack. Slack is what helps you arrive quickly but with an unbroken neck.

32

Learning to Live with Risk

WE GREW UP in an age where stasis was a possibility and a desired state. Change was something you went through to reach a new and better stasis. We may have found such change temporarily unsettling or even unpleasant, but we knew that eventually it would be over and done with. We knew we could soon settle back to enjoy a longish period of reaping the benefits of the change. During that period, disruptive change would only be a memory. Well, those times are over.

The difference between the early nineties and today is the difference between Lenin's concept of revolution (destroy the old state and replace it with a new and better one) and Trotsky's concept of *continuing* revolution (destroy the old state and also destroy each successive state that replaces it). In our new economy, stasis is nothing more than an object of nostalgia. We might look back at it fondly, as we look back at the pre-nuclear age, but we can never go there again.

In times of stasis, risk is an unwelcome visitor. But today risk is a constant. Nobody is ever going to succeed again without constantly taking on risks. And yet, surprisingly, risk avoidance is everywhere.

Risk Avoidance

Risk avoidance is flight from opportunity. As you read these lines, someone in your company is starting a new initiative to do something the company has done a thousand times before. It may be another client-server conversion, or a minor upgrade to plug a slightly faster chip into an existing processor, or a pro forma redesign of last year's vehicle with last year's engine and last year's transmission but a new dashboard layout and different fenders. These "initiatives" are virtually risk-free . . . so it's time to stop doing them.

The only new initiative you can afford to take on today is one that is full of risk. It's got to be something that thrusts you into a new market or exploits a brand-new technology, one that transforms your company at the same time that it transforms your clients and the way they work. If you identify any project as risk-free, or even relatively risk-free, cancel it. You're going to need the resources and calendar time to do something transformational. And you will never get those resources or that time unless you stop doing the nontransformational work.

If you're doing some work that *could* be done without real risk management, that, too, is a clue that you need to redirect your resources. If risk management seems like overkill, you may be in full risk-avoidance mode. It's true you don't need risk management to come up with slightly swervier fenders or a new dashboard clock. But that is not an indictment of the technique; it's an indictment of your overall strategy.

But Aren't We Already Doing Risk Management?

Since you know already—in your bones if not in your head—that risk-taking is a modern-day must, you might be inclined to persuade yourself that risk management must already be in place in your company. You might be inclined to think that it's what you've been doing all along. After all, you are paid to manage in an age of risk, and how else would you do that except by managing the risks?

Even if you're not practicing risk management yourself, you may have convinced yourself that it must be going on somewhere beneath you in the company. Again the logic is the same: We're paying these folks to manage projects and new endeavors that are full of risks, so whatever they're doing must be risk management. But it often isn't. It is often stasis-derived management applied to work where there is no stasis in sight.

The main component of stasis-derived management is what I call a *production mentality.* It is evident in the way managers talk. Here I am not referring to people who manage the assembly line, but people who manage development efforts. They will tell you about building a development "factory" (production word), about "measuring" its "throughput" (both measuring and throughput are production concepts), about "process" (production concept), about "quality control" (production again), about "efficiency" and "return on investment" and "waste management" and "cost reduction" (all valid concepts for dealing with relative stasis). These are the signs of risk avoidance, of failing to get on with the business of the twenty-first century.

In the following section, I offer a test of whether real risk management is happening in your organization. It's a hard test. Most companies fail it. But it's a fair test. I think you can see that an organization that fails the test—or any part of it—is really not managing its risks, and is therefore probably not taking nearly enough risks.

Risk Management: The Hard Test

Pick a part of your company where the risks are greatest. It might be a scary project, one that the company's future depends upon. It might be a new product development or a launch into untried markets. Now apply to it the following hard questions:

❑ Is there a published census of risks? Does the list contain the major causal risks, not just the few outcome risks that we all fear? Is the risk list visible to all who are working on the project? Are there enough risks on the list to indicate careful risk analysis?

❑ Is there a mechanism in place to elicit discovery of new risks? Is it safe for all involved to signal a risk?

❑ Are any of the risks on the list potentially fatal? Risk management that concentrates only on risks that can be handled makes a mockery of the notion of risk management. It's the fatal ones that need your most careful attention.

❑ Is each risk quantified as to probability and cost and schedule impact?

❑ Does each risk have a transition indicator allocated to it to spot materialization? Is each transition indicator being monitored?

❑ Is there a single person responsible for risk management? Where the attitude is that everybody is responsible for managing risks, nobody is responsible for it, since all those people have got Real Work on their plates.

❏ Are there tasks on the work breakdown structure that might not have to be done at all? The absence of such conditional tasks is a sure sign of no risk management at work.

❏ Does the overall effort have both a schedule and a goal, where the schedule and the goal are markedly different? If the schedule is the goal, there is no risk management at work. The earliest date by which the work could conceivably be done makes an excellent goal but an awful schedule.

❏ Is there a significant probability of finishing well before the estimated date? If there is not—if there is no reasonable probability of finishing 20 or 30 percent ahead of schedule— the schedule is a goal, not an estimate.

There it is: my nine-point indicator of whether risk management is being practiced in your organization. They all count. You need to be able to say yes to all of them in order to pass.

Don't be discouraged if you can't answer yes to one or two of the questions; that just means you have some work to do. On the other hand, you should be very discouraged if you can't say yes to most of them. Companies that can't name their risks, that can't distinguish between goals and estimates, are in risk-avoidance mode, or they are taking risks blind. Neither is a good indicator.

Afterword

My unveiling of *Slack* has been, at least in part, a diatribe against efficiency. I hope this hasn't given you the sense that efficiency doesn't matter at all, only that it doesn't matter *most* of all.

The fable of the Needle in the Haystack, which follows, is meant to provide a balanced perspective on the subject. It suggests that if efficiency wins you one point in the Grand Scheme of Things, then a bit of slack, plus some inventiveness, ingenuity, risk-taking, and insight into human relations has the potential to win you three.

At the beginning of the fable, there is a simple and definite goal. At the end, that goal has been achieved. That sounds good but for one tiny fact: The real goal has changed along the way. Will the protagonist, our hero, be agile enough to pick up on the new (much more exciting) goal and work effectively to achieve it? Don't count on it.

33

The Needle in the Haystack

THERE ONCE WAS a young tailor who chanced to lose a needle in a haystack. He searched and searched for it, but to no avail. (In fact, he searched for quite a long time, but I skip over this part in the interest of brevity.)

Being of a philosophical bent, he considered, as he searched, the abstract of the matter. He looked to see if this might be a single instance of a larger class of problem. Sure enough, he realized almost at once that the heart of his present dilemma lay in the superfluity of an obscuring element: The population of hay is large compared to the population of needles. Of course, there could be a boundless set of such problems, all of them at least abstractly identical to his own.

Let n, he thought, represent the number of needles, where n is equal to one in this case. And let h represent the number of discrete pieces of hay. Now, for h larger than n, the difficulty of finding the n can be arbitrarily high. Looked at another way, the probability, P, of finding n goes down as h increases. In fact, there is no number, *delta* (no matter how small), that is not greater than *P* for sufficiently large *h*.

In proceeding through this logic, the young man was discovering what our later era would call the Goldblatt Conjecture, essential to the science of fractals and Mandlebrot sets. But of this, he was unaware. He was a tailor. While he had solved the relationship between *P, h, n,* and *delta,* he was no closer to solving the underlying problem, since he still couldn't find the needle.

As luck would have it, there happened to be knocking about that very haystack at that very moment a lovely young princess. Normally, the tailor would have minded his own business, not even dared to raise his eyes to look at her. But then he had an inspiration:

"Say," he said, "I see that you are a beautiful princess, and I know a thing or two about beautiful princesses."

"Yes," she sighed, "it's an occupational hazard. You aren't in the princess line for more than a few moments before everyone is thinking they know all about you."

"I know, for example, that a princess can feel, even through as many as seven mattresses, that someone has peed in the bed."

"Mm," she said. "You've got some of the details wrong there, but I guess you've caught the essence: We princesses are a sensitive lot."

Then he explained to her about the problem of the needle in the haystack.

"I think I see what you're getting at," she said. "You want me to lie down on this haystack and help you locate your needle."

"Right."

"I'll do it. We should have your needle in a trice. Now, where did you say you lost it?"

"Of that I am not too sure. But somewhere in this general area." And he waved his hands over an expanse of haystack encompassing very large *h.*

"Mm. Well, let's give it a try." With that she plopped down

on a likely spot, wiggled slightly into the hay, and let her eyes drift. "Nope. Not here. Let's give a try over this way."

She moved to a different part of the haystack and lay down again. Again her eyes wandered dreamily. The tailor felt a thumping in his chest. He realized he had never known *anything* about princesses before, at least not about this princess, not a thing. And now . . . Now his life was transformed; it could never be the same again. Where before there was mending and darning, now there was the possibility of Love. His days might be filled with beauty and enchantment, and dancing and cuddling. That was the good part. There was a not-so-good part as well: Where before he had had nothing to lose but a dumb needle, now he had everything to lose. He felt a sudden panic. Oh, above all, don't blow it, he thought.

The princess was frowning. *His* princess was frowning. He felt his rosy new future slipping away. "Well, it's not here either," she said. "I can't understand it."

"No matter, really," the tailor said, too quickly. "Really. It's just a needle."

"But I feel terrible. I feel that I've let you down." She stared up at him sadly from the haystack. She was so beautiful.

"You mustn't, you really mustn't feel so bad. Oh please don't. Even the most sensitive person on earth could be overwhelmed by the sheer numbers here. You see, as the number of pieces of hay (we'll call that h) increases compared to the number of needles, n, the probability, P, of finding n decreases monotonically without limit, and approaches arbitrarily close to zero."

The princess felt something thumping in her own chest. "Wow," she said. "You must be a poet."

"No, a tailor. But please don't feel bad that you have failed."

She sat up on the hay. "Failed? Not me. I just haven't succeeded *yet.*"

"But it's too hard a problem. Please, put it out of your mind. I wouldn't want to be the cause of . . ."

"Nonsense. We'll simply reconstrue. The problem, to find a needle in a haystack, is clearly solvable, even without a princessly backside. All we need to do is to move the h to one side, and everything that is left is n. While h is admittedly large, it is not infinite. The formulation of P, n, and h, which you put so prettily, is static, as it has no temporal element. If we consider instead the dynamic parameter $P(t)$, the probability of finding n among h within a time t, then $P(t)$ increases monotonically toward 1.0 as t increases."

"Yes, but what a t. We're talking eons here," the tailor said glumly. They might be ancient before they could ever get on to the love part.

"So now we reconstrue again." She smiled contentedly at what was about to come, a bit of female logic to finish up the game. "Where you see here a haystack of order h, I instead see a needlestack of order n. Lost in the needlestack are h hays."

"But n is still one and h is still immense!"

"True, but now suppose we search for the h instead of the n. We find the hay lost in the needlestack. Now the numbers are working for us and we're bound to succeed."

The tailor breathed a sigh of relief. "Why couldn't I have seen it that way? What a loser I am."

The princess ignored him and lay back against the hay. "Hello, I've got it," she said at once. She reached under her waist and produced a perfectly splendid piece of hay. "One h. I have succeeded after all. We have succeeded. And now we can get on to other things." She looked up at the tailor, who was rather cute, in addition to being poetic.

But the tailor was staring down at something glittering in the hay. "My needle," he said. And he picked it up triumphantly.

He is a loser, she thought. Can't find a hay in a needlestack, even when the odds are stacked in his favor. She shrugged and went on her way and he never saw her again.

Index

Page numbers of illustrations appear in italics.